Cradled All the While

The Unexpected Gifts
of a Mother's Death

Sara J. Corse

Augsburg Books
MINNEAPOLIS

In loving memory of Jane Kathryn Klein Corse
and Phillip Bonney Corse

and dedicated to their grandchildren
Justin, Phillip, Kalila, Teija, James, and Griffin

CRADLED ALL THE WHILE
The Unexpected Gifts of a Mother's Death

Large-quantity purchases or custom editions of this book are available at a discount from the publisher. For more information, contact the sales department at Augsburg Fortress, Publishers, 1-800-328-4648, or write to: Sales Director, Augsburg Fortress, Publishers, P.O. Box 1209, Minneapolis, MN 55440-1209.

ISBN 0-8066-4644-6

Cover design by Marti Naughton, cover art from Digital Vision
Book design by Michelle L. N. Cook
Author photo by Laurence Salzmann
The poem on pages 73-74 is by Garrie Stevens. Used by permission.

The paper used in this publication meets the minimum requirements of American National Standard for Information Sciences—Permanence of Paper for Printed Library Materials, ANSI Z329.48-1984. ♾ ™

Manufactured in the U.S.A.

08   07   06   05   04   1   2   3   4   5   6   7   8   9   10

Contents

Acknowledgments

To the many people who were present in my mother's life as she was dying, you provided the cradling arms that held us. A special thanks to Kenwyn and our children Justin, Phillip, and Kalila, to my siblings, Kevin and Jennifer, and their families, to my mother's many dear friends, to her sister, Cecily Ann, to the staff, parents and children of the Asbury Day Care Center, and to the many volunteers and health care workers who entered our lives as strangers and left as friends. Without all of you, this book could never have come into being. I include your stories with humility and gratitude.

Many people helped bring this book to fruition. Thanks to fellow writers and readers at Bryn Mawr Presbyterian Church, the University of Pennsylvania and St. Andrews Church in Oxford, England, for encouragement, inspiration, and advice. Thanks to Jennifer Simon for patience, determination, and grace in helping me navigate the complex tangle of memoir-writing. Thanks to Connie Donaldson, Lillian Wall, and Pat Christensen for reading every draft along the way and always finding something new to affirm! Thanks to writing consultant Anne Dubuisson for wise counsel, to my agent, Alice McElhinney, for enthusiastic confidence and to Michael Wilt for envisioning a place for this book at Augsburg Fortress, Publishers.

To Justin, Phillip, and Kalila, thank you for the gift of mothering you—with all your energy, emotions, and ideas—while I was caring for your grandmother. You kept me grounded at the same time that you helped open my eyes to the love in our midst.

To my husband, Kenwyn, thank you for holding the family when I was preoccupied with caring for my mother. Thank you for your unending interest and faith in this book and your steadfast love of its author. Your keen sense of life lived at its most honest and essential enriches this endeavor we call family.

Prologue

October 1997

"Let me see your scratch spin."

My coach begins my weekly figure-skating lesson with the forward one-footed spin, an element I've been struggling to master for months. Some people are natural-born spinners, but I can't find my center. I spiral out of control instead of whirling in place like a top.

"Bring your free leg around with energy.

"Don't leave your right arm behind.

"Stand up, stand up, stand up!" My coach calls out encouragement as I fight for balance.

His suggestions strike me as good advice for more than skating.

As a child I skated on ponds and makeshift rinks, played crack-the-whip and freeze tag with the quick-footed hockey boys, and pretended that I was Peggy Fleming. The winter Peggy took home the gold, my sister, Jen, and I lay on the living-room rug, cradling our chins in our hands and watching the Olympic skating competition. During the commercials we twirled and jumped on the polished wood floor. Our mother, who loved the speed, grace, and poise of figure skaters and ballerinas, egged us on, laughing at our awkward but energetic performance.

"Don't knock my crutches over," Mom's voice dropped an octave in warning as we leapt too close to where they were propped against the doorjamb. My mother hadn't run or danced or skated since collapsing at the bus stop at the age of twenty-one, feverish and aching, a newly graduated Phi Beta Kappa stripped of strength and confidence by polio.

Suddenly alert to our commotion, my father peered at my sister and me over the top of his newspaper, with one eyebrow arched. I paused with the rustling of the paper, ready to claim I'd already stopped whatever it was he disapproved of, while Jen, three years younger than I and naively exuberant, continued to whirl recklessly around the room. But Dad's eyes twinkled as he watched us. He wasn't going to bark. Maybe his ulcer wasn't acting up. Maybe his boss hadn't blamed him for someone else's mistakes today.

I leapt and spun again.

Kevin, my older brother, came up from his basement hideaway, where he worked on model race cars. He plopped on the couch, thumbed noisily through the TV guide in search of something to tempt us away from the ice skating, then sighed in resignation as the commercial ended and Jen and I settled on the floor for the next skater's program.

I dreamt of sit-spins and double axels, was starstruck when the Canadian men's junior champion graced our small town with a performance, and on Friday nights, met my friends at the flooded tennis courts that served as our local ice rink. But with no means or opportunity to pursue skating lessons, my ambitions melted with the ice each spring, and by the time I entered high school, had evaporated completely.

My chance to learn figure skating came nearly thirty years later and quite unexpectedly. A few months after my mother's death, I registered my three young children for hockey and ice-skating lessons at a city rink and learned that a class for adults was scheduled during the same hour. I immediately signed up; then, dodging the puddles on the warming room floor, I exchanged my sneakers for a pair of dull-edged rental skates and prepared to join my classmates on the ice.

We began with basic forward stroking, gliding on one foot and skating backward. I was surprised at how the seemingly minor corrections in body position and weight distribution, suggested by the teacher, dramatically improved my skating. We continued on to learn front and back crossovers and were tackling two-footed spinning when the six-week session ended. By then my earlier passion for skating was rekindled. I approached one of the teachers whom I'd seen at the rink and signed up for private lessons. I learned to refer to him as my coach. I'd had schoolteachers and piano teachers and flute teachers, but never a coach. It was exciting to think of myself as an athlete.

The early days of skating were rich with epiphany for me. It was exhilarating to step onto the ice and be caught up in the joy of movement, to speed around the rink at the far edge of control, and to discover that I had an aptitude for skating. I had never envisioned taking up a dangerous and demanding sport in my late thirties. Though I was vaguely aware as a child that I had athletic potential, I never developed the drive to compete or achieve physically—my involvement in academics, music, and drama often precluded participation in team sports. Suddenly I couldn't get enough of skating—an unknown, unexplored aspect of self was coming to life.

I marveled at the physical abandon I experienced on the ice. As a child I responded to my mother's delight in watching me dance around the house or skip down the street by putting in an extra twirl or hop to make her laugh. But I was aware even then that polio prevented her from experiencing the enjoyment of movement and flow, except vicariously, and I always held something back. With her death the joy of movement was released in me.

I began to recognize that skating is more than just a physical challenge for me; it is a form of meditation and of healing. When I step onto the ice, I forget that I am a mother of three, a psychologist, a grieving daughter. I bring full attention to my bending knees, balanced weight, extended neck. There is no time to hesitate or to entertain the worries of the day when I am preparing to jump in the air or enter the vortex of a spin. A lapse in concentration could mean a broken wrist or a concussion, so I think only of skating. In that clarity of mind and focus on one thing, I am open to bliss; I discover a self that is free from entanglement with the expectations of others or with my need to please.

My skating reflects a deeper search for centeredness off the ice—in my spirit, sense of self, and relationships. I strive to be fully present in each moment, even when surrounded by piles of dirty laundry, clashing egos at work, crowds in a supermarket, or a dispute between siblings. I often fail, losing my center in life's frenzy.

Skating teaches me self-acceptance. It is tempting to compare myself to other skaters, to dwell on my inadequacies, to feel inept. Instead I remind myself that I am a beginner—and with a beginner's mind, I have everything to gain and nothing to lose.

My coach is patient. He knows myriad ways to coax my midlife muscles and soothe my apprehensions. One day he offers a lesson in the physics of spinning. "Remember, a spin is arrested forward movement. As you swing your right side around to the front, your left side has to be there to meet it. The energy collides to send you into the spin. Then you have to hold the center."

I am determined to find and hold the center. I refuse to be disappointed by the large looping coils I etch on the ice, and I try again to carve concentric circles beneath my blades. I practice spinning at home in my socks on the dining-room floor, and when even that is impossible, I spin in my imagination, imperceptibly pressing the ball of my foot to the kitchen floor while peeling potatoes.

"Hold your left side firm," my coach says again and again. "It needs to be there for the right side to meet it. If the left side keeps moving, it will always be out of reach."

The center is never formed; there is only the dance of pursuit.

Off the ice I consider the confrontation of forces that creates a centered spin—accelerating energy encountering a presence holding firm—and I notice how the same dynamic occurs in human relationships. We all need strong holding at times, to be received by someone who isn't derailed by our flailing or floundering but who embraces our energy-in-motion, helping to channel it into our center. It is what a good coach does for an athlete, a teacher for a student, a mentor for a trainee. It is one of the finest gifts a parent can offer a child—steady holding—enough to help her find her center.

I remember my own quiet, aching search for emotional holding from my mother. Somewhere in the seeking, my neediness tapped hers—her anger, anxiety, lack of self-confidence, or frustration—and so began the chasing without catching. Drawn into the swirling eddy of her need, any sense of beginning or ending was lost—I was no longer the pursuer, but the pursued.

To learn how to hold, we must first be held.

The good news is that life offers many opportunities.

My skating coach encourages me to correct my position in the middle of a spin, to find balance and fight centrifugal force even when my entry is off center. He convinces me that it's not too late, and assures me that I'll have as many chances as I need to learn. He draws my attention to the single spot on the quarter-inch slice of metal blade that is the foundation of a spin—the sweet spot, it's called—and urges me to find it and trust it.

The first time I succeed in centering a spin, I find eternity at its core. When forward motion is arrested, time indeed stands still. "Invite the kids in here to join me! Have lunch delivered! I don't ever want to leave this place!" I laugh, giddy with delight.

It is T. S. Eliot's "still point of the turning world."

It is God and love and mystery.

Someday I will learn to center my spins and give over to the wild stillness that forms inside each one. Even when I'm discouraged, convinced that I'll never train my body or tackle my fears, I remember that I have been surprised by grace before.

It was in the midst of turmoil—caring for my mother as she was dying and battling the sharp resurgence of grief for my father's death twenty years before—that I found firm holding, even as I was holding firm. That experience, more than any coincidence of time and place and opportunity, led me into a pair of skates, onto the ice, and on the path to my center.

My mother's final gift to me was given when she was beyond believing that she had anything left to offer anyone, and was received when I was long past expecting anything from her.

Chapter 1

Arrested Forward Movement

January 1996

My mother calls to tell me that they've found a tumor in her abdomen; it's why she's been so tired, anemic, and troubled in the gut. A few days and tests later, and she calls to say that it is malignant; it's going to have to come out. The doctors can't say any more.

The ugly C-word enters my life.

In that shocking moment when you learn bad news, time ceases to behave normally; it stands still or races forward and backward simultaneously. Frozen—frenetic—frantic—the news enters your life and catches you just as you are, with no chance to scrub out or rewrite or revert to what was before.

In what condition am I caught? I have a happy marriage, three beautiful young children, a challenging career, good friends; I sit in the middle of this rosy-cheeked vision of success I present to the world and beam.

Like a ray of sunshine; like Mommy's perfect little girl.

I toddle toward Mommy's smile, my Easter basket clutched in one hand, my bare legs chubby beneath a pink spring coat. Daddy tracks my progress with the movie camera, laughing, encouraging.

Kevin calls out, "Daddy! Mommy! Look at me—watch this!" He moves into the sight line of the camera and prepares to launch a cartwheel—"Here I go. Watch me!"—then dives down and flings his legs overhead. He lands, slightly dizzy, and turns with a proud grin to face his audience.

Mommy, Daddy, and camera, oblivious to Kevin's performance, zoom in on my next footstep.

I am calm on the phone as my mother tells me about the cancer. My own reactions rumble like thunder in the distance, whereas the quaver in her voice is immediate.

"Oh, Mom, I'm so sorry. Are you going to be all right? Do you have plans to be with anyone this evening?" She is crying as I speak. "I wish I could be there with you."

"I'm so upset with this doctor. He's not an easy man to talk to," she complains.

"Would you like me to call him? Should I?"

"Maybe you should. He seemed angry that I live alone. He practically barked at me during my appointment. 'You better get your family here to look after you.'"

"I'll call him. It'll be okay," I reassure, though he has succeeded in inducing guilt.

Staying focused on Mom—what she needs, what she's feeling—I keep my own feelings to myself. That's easy because I don't know yet what they are. Besides, I'm stunned and numb. It's not just the shock. For as long as I can remember, I've tuned into my mother's feelings before my own. It comes so naturally that it must have been bound up in my DNA or written on a star before my birth or absorbed in infancy through the primal sense of smell. Sensing my mother's anxiety swell when I was fretful, shrink when I was calm, and spike and turn to anger when my brother asserted his will, I learned to protect her. I didn't wander too far from her or move too fast, saving her the worry of trying to keep up with me on her crutches. Cheerful and pleasing so her mood wouldn't darken, self-sufficient so her emotional reserves weren't drained, I monitored my mother's emotions without realizing it, without questioning the rightness, without recognizing the cost.

Today I slip back into this way of being with my mother as if I hadn't spent years fighting to throw it off.

The next day I call to check in on Mom, to see how she's doing.

"I'm so upset about what's happening," I blurt out—the first glimpse I give my mother of what I'm feeling—a mild expression of what feels like growing panic.

"You're upset?" Mom snaps back sharply. She seems enraged. "How do you think I feel?"

"Oh, Mom," I answer softly, biting back my anger and the pain of her inability to hear me. "Half the reason I'm upset is because of how upset you must be."

I drag my feelings back inside and squash the wish for a mother's comfort.

The rosy picture of my life is deceptive. Tilt it slightly and, like a hologram, a different image emerges. The outward signs of success and happiness are clouded with a surprising intensity of self-doubt, persistent grief for my father's death, a tense relationship with my mother, the strain of juggling the demands of a full-time career, three young children, and household chores. It is shadowed, too, by the unvoiced experience of that little ray of sunshine: "I need you." "Find out how I feel." "Help me understand."

Mommy lifts her coffee cup to her lips as, across the kitchen table, Barbara does the same. They get together at one house or the other most mornings—after piling the dirty breakfast dishes in the sink and waving their respective children onto the school bus that stops at the corner.

My baby sister is asleep. I don't want to play with Timmy, Barbara's two-year-old. He's too little. I feed my dolly.

Suddenly my name emerges from the background hum of Mommy-chatter. "Sara is always so even tempered and cheerful. But you should have seen her yesterday! I was feeding the baby, and she wanted something, a glass of milk, I think. I said she'd have to wait until I was finished with the baby. Well, she marched over to me and stamped on my foot as hard as she could with her tiny feet, and screeched, 'Right now, Mommy, right now!' It was all I could do to keep from laughing!"

I scowl and hunch my shoulders to block out the Mommy-laughter, tinkling up toward the ceiling.

My mother has cancer. My mother had cancer last month, too, and how long before that?

How could I not know?

I review her recent visit—two weeks in Philadelphia with my family and me for Christmas. Did I miss the signs? She did complain of tiredness and indigestion. She asked me to set up a sleeping space downstairs so she wouldn't have to climb the stairs. She skipped the Christmas Eve church service so she wouldn't be caught needing a bathroom during the service. Still, she took it in stride when we had to walk halfway around The Spectrum, with her on her crutches, to get from the entrance to our seats in the handicapped section at the Disney on Ice show—my miscalculated effort to make the outing easy on her. And several days later, when we arrived at the wrong address for Christmas dinner with friends, she didn't complain about the walk up and down the long sidewalk, but instead laughed at the new euphemism introduced by the woman who met us at the door—resplendent in a plaid kilt, red cashmere sweater, gold bracelets, and diamond rings—then appraised our motley crew with a sweeping glance, and said, "Oh, you must be going to a *family* party!"

We looked at each other and laughed.

We didn't know about the cancer.

Maybe it was our recent habit of downplaying Mom's ailments, taking each as evidence of post-polio syndrome—a constellation of symptoms, including loss of energy, fatigue, and muscle weakness, that affects people who have a history of polio as they age. At first Mom searched for information and new treatments for post-polio syndrome, but found little professional knowledge of—or interest in—this problem that affects a dwindling group of survivors of a nearly eradicated disease. When her health insurance wouldn't cover experimental programs in Pennsylvania and Missouri, she settled for a referral to a local orthopedic specialist. She filled his prescription for a metal and molded-plastic leg brace that extended from heel to hip to support her dragging left foot. She wore the brace once, hated how it felt and how it made her look, and banished it to the dark reaches of her closet. She settled for sporadic attendance at a post-polio support group and bouts of depression over her loss of mobility. Seeing no clear answers to the post-polio problem, I stopped asking questions. But when my husband, Kenwyn, and I renovated the bathroom, we made sure it was handicapped accessible, in case Mom ever needed to live with us.

No, Mom and I didn't focus on her health during her Christmastime visit. I was putting forth extra effort to show her a good time. A few months earlier, she'd complained that I never organized special outings when she came to stay with me, like my sister-in-law does. Embarrassed, I planned a shopping trip, lunch with a friend, the ice show, and the movies. Defensive, I wondered why my usual offerings—the antics of her three grandchildren, an ear for her oft-repeated stories about work and friends, and inclusion in our family routine—didn't represent a full program of entertainment. I wasn't thinking about her medical tests or symptoms.

The surgery to remove Mom's tumor is scheduled for a month from now, and I'm on a crash course to learn about colon cancer. They say that it's one of the slowest growing cancers, that a complete recovery can be expected with early detection and full removal of the tumor. I discover that my maternal grandfather had a cancerous tumor removed from his colon in his early sixties, and lived, albeit with the embarrassment of a colostomy bag, until the age of eighty-five, when he died of a stroke. Armed with this information, I convince myself that my mother will survive.

I call Mom nearly every day. She is tired, has no appetite, and is annoyed with the invasive medical tests. Although she used the word *cancer* once or twice in the beginning, I notice that it's disappearing from her lexicon. Instead she latches onto details of the operation and memories of her father's later years. "Are you sure they can do a resection?" she frets, though the surgeon assures her that he will be able to rejoin the sections of her large intestine once the tumor is removed. "I can't live with a colostomy bag."

I wonder why the doctors aren't running more tests, why they are waiting so long to do the surgery, but I don't say this to Mom. I simply offer encouragement and comfort. I organize plane reservations, work leave, and child care so I can go to Rochester and be with her when she goes into the hospital.

"Turn right!" I urge the taxi driver as soon as I spot an entrance to the hospital. "Just let me out here!"

The plane delay, the wait for luggage, and the traffic have added to my sense of urgency.

It is February 13, 1996, the day before Mom's surgery. It is four hours since I kissed my husband and three young children good-bye in Philadelphia.

Dodging groups of uniformed staff discussing lunch plans, visitors consulting directories, and patients pushing IV poles, I half-walk, half-jog down the hospital hallway toward the admissions desk. Inside my bulky, down-filled jacket, I am sweltering from exertion and the shocking contrast between the frigid Rochester weather and the overheated hospital.

The corridors change from fresh paint and shiny linoleum to yellowed tile, and it dawns on me that I've chosen the furthest entrance from the admissions department. I shift my suitcase from left hand to right, and move my briefcase to loosen the strap that is biting into my shoulder. I am regretting my packing choices. Will I use the laptop computer to work on that months-old, half-written academic paper, read all five books, sit at Mom's bedside and embroider, wear all these sweaters?

The other burdens I shoulder are less tangible: fear, nervous anticipation, a growing sense of responsibility. Despite the heat I'm generating, shivers of anxiety play up and down my spine.

When I find my mother's room at the end of a long corridor, it, too, is charged with nervous energy. Mom and Jen spot me in the doorway, and ring out, "Thank God, you're here!"

Mom seems to glow; her cheeks reflect her rosy red sweater and restrained panic. Black and silver earrings I helped her choose during her visit to the Adirondacks last summer dangle gracefully from her ears. Her hair and nails betray a recent trip to the beauty parlor. We have been preparing, each in our own way. Her wide-eyed look of terror and gratitude enhances her beauty.

Jen grips me as we hug. She has spent the weekend with Mom to help her get through the waiting days before surgery, and is relieved to share the burden with me.

We describe our traveling woes—my flight delays, Jen's near miss on the expressway as she drove Mom to the hospital, my labored trek down the hallways, the drawn-out tedium of admission procedures. We are giddy, retelling every joke and story that we'd used to distract ourselves over the last few days. No one mentions why we're here as we cling to a sense of normalcy.

After this flurry of connecting and catching up, I glance around the room. "This is the best room in the unit!" I remark as

I settle on the couch. It is private and larger than any I had passed along the way.

"Yes, I have friends in high places," Mom announces with a swagger. "Evelyn arranged for this room. She has a daughter at the day-care center, and works here in the hospital as a social worker."

Soon Evelyn drops by to see how Mom is settling in, along with Dawn, another day-care parent, who works at the hospital as a pathologist. They are warm and affectionate with Mom, and I realize that during sixteen years as the office administrator of the Asbury Day Care Center, she's created a vast network of relationships with parents, teachers, board members, and children. Mom plays the gracious hostess, amuses us with one-liners, and fights her apprehension.

A nurse interrupts our little party. She hands Mom a hospital gown and asks her to change out of her street clothes. Off come the red sweater and earrings; on goes a pale blue hospital gown. A laboratory nurse arrives to draw blood for some tests. The bed replaces the chair. The IV nurse searches for a good vein. The floor nurse does preoperative teaching. The TV and telephone man comes by for the first day's rental fee. On goes the TV. A resident turns up to answer questions and describe the preoperative procedures.

Within an hour the glow of Mom's cheeks has faded.

As evening approaches I settle in for my overnight shift in the hospital. I slip out to a nearby Indian restaurant to order a take-out dinner, and wind up chatting with a deliveryman who is also waiting. Ten minutes later I leave the restaurant with Palak Paneer and a greater than necessary appreciation for the deliveryman's joint custody arrangements, while he takes off with Tandoori Chicken and the details of Mom's medical situation.

I eat as much as my nervous energy allows, create a bed out of a reclining chair and the pillows and blankets that I beg from the nursing staff, and watch a television drama with Mom.

At 11:00 PM I am thinking seriously about sleep—that nervous, "night before the first day of school" kind of sleep—when the trauma begins. A nurse arrives, following a schedule to which we are not privy, and asks Mom to drink a gallon of Go-Litely, a fluid designed to empty her colon to reduce the likelihood of infection during surgery. A week ago she had to drink the same liquid in preparation for a medical test.

"I can't do this again," she says dejectedly. "It's vile."

"Just try," I urge, handing her the first cup.

By the end of an hour, Mom has drunk less than a pint of Go-Litely. "My throat has closed up, Sara. I just can't swallow anymore."

"Do I really have to drink this awful stuff?" she asks the medical resident the next time he stops by.

"Yes, you do. But I can make it easier for you with a nose tube."

That idea appeals to her, to send the nasty liquid down the back of her throat, bypassing her taste buds and gag reflex.

We wait more than an hour for the resident to return to insert the tube. Once it is in place, he injects a few ounces into it.

"Now we'll wait for half an hour before we put any more in there."

With unspoken horror I calculate the number of ounces left in the gallon jug of Go-Litely, and project out the number of half-hour intervals before it is empty. We will be up until the wee hours of the morning—we're never going to sleep.

After several hours of injecting and waiting and using the commode and waiting some more, the resident injects the last bit of Go-Litely. "You'll feel a little discomfort," he announces as he prepares to pull out the nose tube.

My mother jerks with the sharp pain, and reflexively moves her hand to catch the drops of blood that fall from her nose. Her eyes meet mine with a look of shock and outrage, like the one my children give me when a nurse jabs in the needle for a vaccination, saying, "This will pinch a little."

We drop into fitful sleep in the early hours of the morning, only to be interrupted by the relentless hospital schedule. The nursing shift changes, medical students, residents, and attending doctors make their rounds, vital signs are checked and rechecked. A new day dawns.

The hours before Mom's surgery drag, even with the TV talk shows turned on for distraction. When Jen arrives I slip out to hunt down a fiber-filled breakfast in the hospital cafeteria, my attention to diet sharpened by the condition of Mom's colon. Fat, sugar, cholesterol, and refined flour are in abundance. After a long search, I discover a tray of oatmeal congealing on the steam table. A hefty spoonful of brown sugar helps it go down.

I pass the meditation room on the way back from the cafeteria and consider going in. It's a place for silence and prayer, for comfort. But I would only be pretending if I sat there and bowed my head. I'd be more likely to encounter my own confusion and ambivalence about faith than God's loving presence. Besides, despite a desperate urge to escape Mom's room twenty minutes ago, I am now desperate to return, afraid that Mom needs me. The feeling registers as a swell and an ache in my breasts, though my youngest child is five years old and long past nursing.

Finally, staff arrive to wheel Mom to surgery. She complains that the drug given to calm her down isn't working. "Why can't they just knock me out?" she asks. She is ushered into a preoperative waiting area; a nurse checks her pulse and blood pressure and eases her onto a gurney. The wait is long. Jen and I stand on either side of the bed, rubbing her hands, which are getting colder, and offer words of encouragement. "Everything is going to be all right," I assure her. I am surprised to hear the conviction in my voice.

"The surgery will take two hours or more," the nurse tells us after Mom is wheeled away. "You can wait in the main hospital lobby. The surgeon will look for you there when they've finished."

Jen and I try the lounge; family groups are clustered in corners of the large public space or pacing the passageways. Worry coats the dull upholstery like fine dust. "Let's get out of here and find some fresh air," I suggest.

The hospital is in one of Rochester's oldest neighborhoods; quaint shops and restaurants line the main street. Windows filled with hearts and angels announce Valentine's Day. It is snowing gently.

Jen and I wander in and out of the stores, fingering the fabric of dresses on mannequins, picking up knickknacks and checking prices without registering the numbers on the tags. I notice the things that we are drawn to, and, as always, I'm fascinated by our differences. Jen, dark-haired where I am fair, is attracted to the exotic and earthy. She's willing to experiment while I never stray far from the classic and sensible.

It wasn't easy for my little sister to follow in my straight and narrow footsteps as a child, to face the teachers who remembered my A's and good behavior, or to live with my finely honed ability to anticipate what was wanted at home and deliver it before it was asked for—or just before the not-delivering was noticed and punished. "As different as night and day," Mom always said, and we both knew that day was better. Praised for being sunny and even tempered, I was both attracted to and disturbed by my sister's dark moods and expressiveness; I exploited her emotional vulnerability at the same time that I distanced myself from it.

"Sara, be nice to Jenny," Mom once said. "Remember, Grandma doesn't like her as much as she does you." I knew that I should be nicer. I should stop encouraging my sister in mischief, then abandoning her to take the punishment alone; I should protect her more. But our mother's comments during early childhood kept us from knowing and loving each other; they fed my sense that I was better, in a way that reminded me that I was not.

Still, there were stretches of time when my sister and I shared secrets, made each other laugh, and entertained each other with stories. During college and graduate school, when Jen struggled with depression, self-hatred, bad relationships, or conflict with Mom, she called me, her budding psychologist big sister, for advice and support. I tried to be there for her.

In recent years our relationship is more mutual as Jen finds her own strengths and I grow to appreciate them. I am emboldened when I watch her interact with Mom these days. She doesn't withdraw from Mom's anger or complaints the way I do, but stays with her until she's moved through those feelings and is more receptive to help. She is assertive, yet accepting of

Mom's emotional flailing, and has strong faith in the guidance she can offer her.

It is lunchtime, and Jen and I stop at a small deli to order sandwiches. We are both drawn to the same item on the menu, perhaps by the same longing for familiarity and comfort. But we're surprised when we unwrap our sandwiches. "This doesn't look like Mom's egg salad!" I exclaim. We giggle hysterically as whole black olives, planted in the chopped egg like tulip bulbs, threaten to pop out with every bite.

Worry about the time suddenly interrupts our brief levity. We eat our chocolate kiss cookies during the hurried walk back to the hospital.

In the lobby we find Connie, one of Mom's closest friends, waiting for us. She has always maintained strong relationships with me and Jen and Kevin, apart from her relationship with Mom, and she often serves as behind-the-scenes mediator. She's come straight from the airport, returning from a psychotherapy conference in the Midwest.

Within a few minutes, we spot the surgeon walking toward us, his expression sober and tense.

"I'm afraid the news is not good," he launches in without ceremony. "Your mother's cancer has spread beyond her colon to her omentum, the lining of the abdomen. We took out what we could, but it has metastasized to the liver."

As tears stream silently down my face, I lose track of some of his words—those that come through, I don't like.

"Incurable . . . months left . . . and I emphasize months . . . a year at the outside."

We try to hold the surgeon with our questions, to delay the moment when we are alone with this shocking news, but he moves briskly through his litany, curtly addresses our concerns, and exits.

Jen, Connie, and I stay rooted on the couch, locked in a tearful embrace, oblivious to the other people in the lounge who withdraw instinctively from our pain. Reluctantly letting reality sink in, we repeat everything that the surgeon has said, filling in for one another the details we missed on first hearing.

A feeling of dread grows thick and huge inside of me.

"No, no, no, I can't," I moan quietly to myself. "I can't go through this again! Don't take my mother."

We aren't allowed to see Mom while she's in the recovery room. Taking over the phone booth near the nurses' station, we call Kevin, then our husbands and a close friend or two. I thought I'd grasped the surgeon's report, but as I report his words to others, my mental armor fractures; the full horror of it seeps through the cracks, and I sob.

When Mom is wheeled back to her room on a stretcher, I feel like hiding. How can I face her questions and reactions and give her what she needs? "Leave the telling to me," the surgeon had insisted. "I'll give her as much information as she wants—but only when she asks me." We are unlikely to see him again before tomorrow's morning rounds.

Mom doesn't ask any questions, but her eyes search ours for reassurance. We rush in with hollow enthusiasm. "The surgery went fine. They were able to do a bowel resection; you won't have to use a colostomy bag. They say you did great." I'm on tenterhooks, worried that she'll formulate a direct question and I won't know what to say. I busy myself fetching ice and blankets, making phone calls, consulting with a nurse. I only settle down when I realize that Mom is too frightened and sedated to ask for information.

The evening news gives way to game shows and then prime time, nurses bustle in and out, Mom drifts on a morphine cloud. Connie, watching Jen and me slowly deflate with shock and fatigue, offers to spend the night at the hospital.

"Connie can't hear a thing when she takes her hearing aid off." Mom is suddenly alert to our impending abandonment of her. "What kind of help will she be? She sleeps like a log!" But Jen and I extricate ourselves from the tangled strands of grief, confusion, and guilt that booby-trap our path to the door, and leave for Mom's town house on the outskirts of Rochester.

The thirty-six hours since I've left Philadelphia feel more like thirty-six weeks. The world outside the hospital is unrelentingly regular—the chill in the air, the musty smell of the car, the traffic lights turning from amber to red show no regard for what is happening to our family.

At Mom's house we find her answering machine blinking crazily—nine messages from friends and relatives who want to know about the surgery. This day is not yet over.

"What are we going to tell everyone?" Jen asks.

"I don't know. It doesn't seem right for other people to find out how bad it is when Mom doesn't know yet."

We call Kevin for a consultation, and together we decide not to mention diagnosis or prognosis when we talk to others. "She's resting comfortably" will have to suffice for now.

I don't feel easy about this evasion. Maybe it's because I've already weathered the death of a parent, or maybe I've adopted my mother's pet peeves. She hates euphemistic references to death or disease, and so do I. No one in the family fails to spot a bad comb-over either, perhaps as a way to applaud Dad's graceful acceptance of early baldness. People shouldn't shy away from the harsh reality of death, is what I learned at home. I think. People should be proud to be bald. I don't think the rule of directness or proud acceptance has ever applied to walking with crutches, not really.

Anyway, I get on the phone and spout platitudes. "Jane is doing fine. She's alert and not too uncomfortable. We won't know more until the pathology report comes in," I spin the agreed-upon story.

Jen marvels at my calm. "You seem so confident, so able to find innocuous words to describe the appalling."

Maybe it's my training in empathy—professional and otherwise. With each call I make, I imagine the reaction of a sister, a girlhood pal, a bridge partner, a colleague, or a friend to the loss of their Jane. I am so preoccupied with the pain of others that I barely notice how they reach out with concern to me, a daughter who will lose her mother.

After I talk with the people on our list, I call Kenwyn. He is alert to my mood, familiar with my tendency to focus on everyone's feelings but my own. "What are you going to do to take care of yourself?" he asks.

"I've been faking it through all these phone calls, pretending that things are going to be fine when they're not. I need to tell the real story to someone who doesn't need the censored version." I mention a new friend I'd like to call, a minister at our Presbyterian church. "She's so busy, though, and it's nearly eleven o'clock. Isn't it too late to call?"

"Go ahead," Kenwyn encourages. "Take a risk."

Pattie assures me that I can call her anytime. I burst into tears when I tell her that my mother is going to die. "I've already been through a heart-attack death with my father," I moan. "Why do I have to go through a cancer death, too? It's too much. It will be my undoing."

This phrase has been on my mind all evening, along with images of how people unravel and come undone. They withdraw, become anxious, cling to what they have so that nothing else can be taken from them; their lives are shaped by grief. How will I find the emotional strength to hold my mother together through this final stage of life? Who will hold me together?

"Will you pray for me?" I ask Pattie as our conversation comes to a close. "I don't really know how to pray. I just want to listen to you."

I close my eyes and let the tears trickle down my cheeks as I listen to Pattie's rich, expressive voice. "Wrap Sara and her family in your loving arms. Bring them peace and sleep."

I try to imagine the feeling of those arms as I give over to exhaustion.

Chapter 2
Beginnings

I awake in my parents' king-sized bed—Mom hasn't been able to part with it since Dad died. A thunk in the gut reminds me that something is wrong before my mind can wrap itself around a single thought.

Then it hits. My mother is going to die.

Confronted with her mortality, surrounded by her possessions, my mother's life seems to condense and fold in on me. As I shower, dress, eat breakfast, clean the kitchen, and empty the garbage, I am drawn to her things, the stuff of her life; I touch them. Is it to hold the overwhelming notion of her death at bay or to make it real?

Like an archaeologist on a dig, I mentally rope off sections of the town house, sift through layers, catalogue findings.

The first stratum reflects the emotional chaos of recent days—the kitchen bears witness to comfort food—ice cream, rice pudding, chocolate. An end table in the living room is topped with candles, precious stones, and incense—a makeshift altar where Jen prayed for healing. The coffee table holds items of distraction—books, crossword puzzles, videotapes, the TV listings.

Beneath this surface clutter is a mixture of the familiar and the unknown. Polaroid photos of Jen and Kevin and me during the gawky teenage years, Dr. Seuss books, the antique mantle clock, the old washstand, the Hoosier cabinet; school pictures of my children, in frames that I helped them make for their grand-mother's birthday last year. Newer items consistent with the mother I have known—coffee-table books on JFK and the Vietnam Veterans Memorial, piles of unread paperback books in every corner, the result of Mom's decision to give up lending libraries and buy all the books that catch her eye in the *New York Times Book Review*. And there are the collectibles: apples made of crystal, copper, or ceramic; eggs of polished stone; mugs from around the world; anything about whales—gifts from so many. Had I noticed their proliferation, I might have added to them at birthdays and Mother's Days, instead of resorting to Teleflora at the last moment.

I move on to a deeper layer of history, visible when I open closets, cupboards, and drawers. My Grandma Corse's good china, Grandma Klein's sewing machine, fabric remnants from three generations of sewing projects, family photos and letters, my father's shaving brush, the Mickey Mouse mug that I won in eighth-grade speech class, Mom's purple velvet wedding dress, costume jewelry I raided as a teenager, a furry smiley-face sticker from the 1970s coming unstuck at the edges, my mother's despised leg brace.

They are the artifacts of a human life—the story of my fam-ily—my inheritance.

Boxes of photos and letters hold my mother's life story from before I was born. There is a small snapshot of my mother, Jane, and her sister, Cecily Anne, or Cis, standing with their mother outside the apartment building in which they grew up in Hyde Park, Chicago, during the Great Depression. Jane, at two or three, stands on sturdy toddler legs, holds the hand of her ele-gant mother, and laughs at the camera. I want to laugh, too, to lift this little girl and swing her around in a circle until we are both giggling. Cis, older by two years, has skinny legs and smiles uncertainly; I would be more cautious with her. Although busi-ness at their father's cigar shop is slow, their mother knows how to stretch the money, and will soon find work as a bookkeeper.

In another photo, Jane, Cis, and their cousins, Elrita and Joanne, wear matching sunsuits and line up according to age on the steps of a cottage at Gages Lake. Aunt Elsie and Uncle Hilmer look after the girls there each summer while Inez and Leo, my mother's parents, work in Chicago, visiting on weekends when they are able. Jane is strikingly beautiful. She stands out as the most athletic and spunky.

Jane and Elrita are cousins the same age, and close friends. A stack of letters, tied with a blue ribbon, attests to their active correspondence during the teenage years. With Jane in Chicago and Elrita in nearby Waukegan, they write every week of the movies they see, clothes they covet, friends they share. World War II has little effect on them, it seems. Aside from an occasional mention of rationing or the shortage of money for a new dress or pair of shoes, and episodes of sock knitting and bandage rolling, the only feeling of true deprivation comes one summer when Elrita's family can't afford to rent a cottage big enough to accommodate Jane and Cis at Gages Lake. They spend the summer at home in the Chicago heat, undoubtedly staying away from public swimming areas for fear of the crippling polio virus.

Jane's well-worn scrapbooks from high school and college display her twinkling eyes, party dresses with cinched waists and wide skirts, blue jeans with cuffs rolled up to midcalf, giggling girlfriends arm in arm, smiles shared with a handsome boyfriend, and waving mortar boards at graduations. Along with the photographs are mementos: dance cards, invitations to sorority events, notice of her induction into Phi Beta Kappa, a college diploma that reads *magna cum laude* with a BA in psychology—years of vitality and accomplishment neatly tucked into two volumes.

There are piles of letters between Jane and her parents. One written on Dec. 5, 1945, is from Inez just before she leaves to spend six weeks with her own aging parents. She offers Cis, age nineteen, and Jane, seventeen, advice on schooling, marriage, and right living. She describes her daughters' different strengths, and doesn't hide her admiration and high expectations of my mother.

She points out their Achilles' heels. The letter was written "just in case," and not delivered until many decades later:

> Dear Girls,
>
> I'm writing this letter before I go away, but you may never see it.
>
> I want you to know how much I love you, and besides that, I adore both of you, and you and Daddy are what I live for. . . .
>
> Cecily Anne, keep your unselfish disposition, but keep trying to take responsibility for your own life and living, doing your just share of work and planning. It is hard for you, but the sooner you learn to do the difficult and unpleasant things first, the better off you will be and the more time you'll have to really enjoy your relaxation.
>
> Jane, you don't need advice about doing things, and I hope you will continue through your whole life to do the many things you are capable of doing, and don't criticize others for not keeping up with you. You have exceptional ability, and could no doubt go far if you desired. Don't spoil things for yourself by setting too-high standards for others to live up to; most people are unable to arise to the heights you will reach, and they resent being made to realize it. . . .
>
> Lovingly, Mother

Jane writes letters to her parents during college, forthright in asking for what she needs. "It's beginning to get cold here, Mother, so if you wouldn't mind sending my green coat down, along with my sweaters" and "I could really use some more money, whenever you can send it. You know how I hate to ask."

There is a gap of at least a year in the flow of letters and pictures, but I can fill in the story from what I've heard. First a chapter on uncertain ambitions: Jane is urged by a favorite professor to pursue an advanced degree in psychology and to work as his research assistant. She takes a summer job in the medical school library while she considers her options. Next, a shocker: Jane falls desperately ill in the heat of August; poliomyelitis causes irreparable nerve damage to her legs and toes. She spends the next nine months in a rehabilitation hospital, painfully stretching her muscles, and relearning how to walk, her spirits buoyed by nurses, physical therapists, and the other patients, who become her friends.

After leaving the hospital, Jane returns to her parents' home. She continues to progress in physical therapy, but struggles with the dawning realization of her limitations and battles with her mother—who alternates between being overprotective and overly demanding, asking the impossible of Jane's damaged legs. Jane casts about for a return to independence. When Jane's letters to her parents resume, they are postmarked Missoula, Montana, where she has gone to visit Elrita, who is pursuing a master's degree in English at the University of Montana. Excerpts from those letters hint at how her physical handicap affects her lifestyle.

March 1952

Dear Folks,

. . . We went to the show twice this week—saw *An American in Paris,* with John and then last night we went out alone with the wheelchair (in a small snowstorm) to see *Phone Call from a Stranger.*

That sled we have really gives me a pain in the neck. I never wanted it, and E. insisted on getting it, and then we have used it exactly three times. She paid $7.50 for it, and I have never repaid her. Maybe I will try to sell it before I leave. Fat chance at this time of year. I am really slightly bitter about the whole sled business.

. . . [My train] is due in at 1:45, but might very well be late, as eastern Montana and North Dakota are snowbound. And please, no wheelchair at the station. I'll make it even if I have to crawl, and I was aroused to maniacal fury when I saw it there at Christmastime. So let's start my new session at home on good terms.

April 1952

Dear Folks,

   . . . I have felt plenty sorry for myself in the past two years,
but it has suddenly occurred to me that I can also be a little
proud of the way I faced up to the things that happened to
me. . . .

Jane's crutches are often absent in photographs taken in the
years just after polio, though they can't be far away. I have
scanned those photos before, searching each picture for the familiar wooden sticks with the leather bands and rubber tips—often
finding them missing. Are those her crutches at the edge of the
photo, not quite out of sight? Are they behind her with the tips
visible below her coat? Is that them, casting a shadow on the
snow? Without her crutches how does she keep her balance for
the photographer? Is she leaning against that railing? Is that man
propping her up? Did she link arms with girlfriends to steady her?

   It troubles me that she takes pains to conceal what I most
want to know.

   There is a picture of Phillip Corse in his army uniform—my
mother's knight in olive drab. She is living in Chicago with her
parents again, working as a secretary, when she meets Phil at a
social event for enlisted men who are stationed at Fifth Army
Headquarters during the Korean War. He is drawn to the dark-
haired beauty with the sardonic wit who trounces him in a game
of Scrabble. She finds him handsome and engaging, though an
atrocious speller. Her crutches, at first tucked discreetly beneath
her chair and later slipped over her coat sleeves and gripped in
each hand, do not appear to alarm him.

   It is a brief courtship; soon Phil professes his love. Jane's
blunt response belies her strong attraction to this confident, caring man. She doesn't reply with, "I love you, too," though she is
quite sure that she does. Instead she asks, "What are you planning
to do about it?" and recounts the two broken engagements—the
men who couldn't envision marrying a handicapped woman. "I
don't want to go through that again," she cautions.

"Then let's forget the engagement and just get married," he suggests.

A letter from Phil's father, George, sent from his small home-town in northern New York, expresses surprise at how quickly Jane and Phil decide to marry.

> Dear Phil—and Jane—Because that is the way it will be from now on!
>
> Flabbergasted plenty, but thoroughly approving we will come. Naturally we were both almost speechless, but we knew you would sometime pick a girl in a million—and Jane, we are thoroughly convinced that you do likewise, for Phil is "tops" here in this his hometown.
>
> Certainly we will be glad to see our son and daughter together as one.
>
> Your Dad
>
> P.S. I called Mary Lou, and she said "Holy Smoke, Holy Cow, Omigosh!!"

In the same envelope are scraps of paper with quotes written in Jane's hand. Her sentiments about getting married? about being crippled by polio?

> "She was to him what no one has been to me, the one person in the world—from whom nothing is held back."
>
> "It's what I want, a choice. To know I could've had another life, all made of my own decisions. That would be making my peace and truly."
>
> *The Grass Harp,* Truman Capote (Random House, 1951)

The wedding album shows a simple ceremony, with the two families and one friend each for the bride and groom, in Jane's parents' apartment. It is mid-September. Jane's off-the-shoulder purple velvet dress has three-quarter-length sleeves, a tight bodice, and a full skirt falling to midcalf. Her new

brother-in-law, Dave, a lanky sixteen-year-old, looks uncomfortable in a suit. The couple beams.

Jane and Phil settle in an apartment in Chicago, and a year
later have their first child, Kevin. Kevin's baby album records his
earliest days: wailing on the diaper-changing table, nestled in his
father's arm wearing matching nightshirt and hat, looking at the
world with wide-eyed wonder. The background of the pictures
changes as the young family moves several times after Phil is discharged from the army. He finds work in a mining company, a
string of administrative jobs that take the young family from
Chicago to Nevada to New Mexico to Montana in the space of
three years. They struggle financially, and Phil rapidly assumes an
ambivalent attitude toward company life at the lower rungs. With
restless ambition he dreams up schemes for self-employment
with the same passion with which he rails against the conformity
and complicity required to play the advancement game in an
exploitative corporation. He develops his first ulcers.

Meanwhile Jane seeks friends among the company wives and
neighbors, looking for opportunities to play bridge and chat over
morning coffee while toddlers and babies play nearby. She quietly
worries that a woman who is unable to chase after her children and
snatch them from danger shouldn't take on the responsibility of
motherhood. Her general anxieties about being a mother and handicapped seem to fixate on the fact that her firstborn is a boy. She
complains that she doesn't know what to do with Kevin, and as he
develops energy, interests, and opinions of his own, they enter a battle of wills. "Love him. He's a baby; just love him," Phil encourages.

"I was the second daughter of one of three sisters, with four
female cousins. There were no boys in my family. What did I know
about raising a boy?" Jane says much later, by way of explanation.

In Montana I join Kevin in family pictures. A baby with flaxen
hair that sticks straight up—"like a dandelion gone to seed," my
mother likes to say—I seem to be sprinkled with sunshine. I am
unaware of the hopes awaiting my birth, don't know what it
means that I am a girl—easy to please and pleasing—the baby
that my mother was expecting from the first.

I come to know my favored position in the family, experiencing its nuances before I can talk. It is confirmed in Jane's letter to her parents, written when I am almost seven months old:

Feb. 1, 1959
Dear Folks,
     . . . It is noon on Sunday. Phil and Kevin have gone skiing and Sara is asleep. . . . I long for the summertime when Kevin can play out all day. Sara alone is no trouble at all. (How overworked I thought I was when Kevin was that age!) Of course, I have the playpen for Sara, which is wonderful. She can scoot all around it now on her tummy, and can roll over both ways, so she is quite self-sufficient in the pen. Kevin also gets in it and plays with her. She is in paradise when he plays with her, and lets him haul her and maul her to his heart's content. Did I ever tell you about the time, about a month ago, when I was in the kitchen and looked up and there was Kevin, carrying Sara in from the bedroom? I was so startled I just stood there saying, "Oh, Kevin!" He didn't drop her, and she was quite insulted when I finally got over to them and picked her up by one arm and one leg. She's getting so fat, and is still a marvelous eater. What a change from when Kevin was a baby. I think that is when we got off on the wrong foot with each other. . . .

And when I am two, she writes:

Sept. 18, 1960
Dear Folks,
     . . . The only excitement last week was that Sara got her hand caught in the car door, and had to have six stitches taken in the third finger of her right hand. Can you imagine six stitches in one of those tiny fingers? It didn't slow her down much, though, and she never thinks of it now except to reproach me once in a while with "you slammed the door on my finger" . . .

This letter, and the photos and letters to follow, jog my early memories. I remember the accident with the car door. I felt free to remind my mother of her role in it, scowling as I made my accusation, scowling more deeply at my mother's half-veiled, guilt-ridden amusement at my display of anger and assertiveness.

Another event that occurred around the same time was never retold in the family. My memory of it is primitive, free of the layers of interpretation that grow around a story that becomes family lore.

> *Kevin is being bad. He won't pick up his toy gas station.*
> *Mommy told him to do it a lot of times.*
> *She is screaming out the window at him.*
> *I am playing and watching Kevin practice somersaults.*
> *Mommy is coming outside. Oh, is she mad! She's smashing Kevin's gas station with her crutches and yelling. The cars are flying. The metal is crunching. I don't like this.*
> *My teddy is upside down from a somersault. I better get him.*
> *Mommy is bashing and bashing the gas station. She made it flat.*
> *I am small and quiet. I can hold my breath. I'm not crying.*
> *Teddy better sit up straight.*
> *Mommy is shouting some more.*
> *I am crying.*
> *My daddy has a gas station. He works really hard.*
> *Mommy doesn't like it when he gets home late.*
> *I like the way his hands smell when he comes home.*

Kevin started first grade that September, with children nearly a year older than he was. When Mom learned that the local elementary school had no kindergarten program, and that Kevin's birthday fell after the cutoff date for enrollment in the first grade, she was dismayed. Unable to imagine another year of locking horns with her energetic and determined son, and convinced that he needed outside stimulation, she and Dad altered his birth certificate so he could begin school early.

When Kevin was five-and-a-half and I was almost three, our sister, Jennifer, was born. It was an unplanned conception, according to our mother. But when Dad overheard her describe it that way, he interjected: "Oh, no. She was planned—I planned her." At which point Mom would rephrase it, saying that she had always wanted three children, "just not that particular month." By the time we were adults, Mom acknowledged that she had been furious at Dad. She blamed him for taking chances, for not talking it through together, but, paralyzed by her sense of dependency, she never told him. "How could I tell him, and risk angering the very person I might have to turn to a minute later and ask for help?" Instead her anger seeped out in interaction with the baby. It didn't help that my sister nearly died of dehydration after a serious stomach bug at three months old—threatening to enact my mother's worst fear. It didn't help that my sister came into the world harboring the passions and depth of feeling of a poet.

Though my mother appeared to cope well, she had difficulty accepting her children as three complete and complex emotional creatures. She had trouble weathering the reactions we stirred in her.

In the midst of this family stew, I was even-tempered and independent, yet vigilant. Craving closeness, keeping distant.

Mommy wants to tell me about the birds and the bees.

I've already heard, and I don't care.

She tells her friends that I never ask any questions, that I won't even look at her when she talks about it.

Not like Kevin, who asked a lot of questions when he was even littler than me.

"And then Kevin asked how the sperm gets to the egg. When I told him that the daddy puts it in the mommy with his penis, Kevin shouted, 'You mean he squirts it in?'"

Mommy always tells the story the same way, and laughs and laughs.

When she makes me listen to all that stuff, I don't have to cover my ears; I can shut them from inside.

I shake my head when she asks if I have any questions, and I ask if I can go outside.

I was almost five when we moved from Montana to Sandy Creek, New York, Dad's hometown. Maybe my parents had been considering such a move, but my grandfather's sudden death from a heart attack at age sixty-four triggered it. Dad wanted to be closer to his mother and grandmother and brother so he could look after them. Dad and Kevin drove cross-country in the pickup truck loaded with all our possessions, while Mom and Jen and I took the train, spending the night in narrow bunk beds in a sleeper car. For the first several weeks, we lived with Grandma Corse and Great-Grandma Bonney in the house where my father grew up. Then we rented a house on a country road dotted with dairy farms to the east of town. Summer was over, and it was time for me to start school.

Kevin and I stand at the end of the driveway, waiting for the school bus. It is the first day of school, kindergarten for me, third grade for Kevin. When the bus arrives, Kevin jumps aboard, and I stretch my legs to reach the big steps behind him. There are no seats for two on the bus, and Kevin has already gone toward the rear, grabbing the seat backs as the bus lurches forward. I sit quickly in the nearest empty seat.

When the bus pulls into Sandy Creek Central School, elementary teachers pluck the youngest children from the crowd and lead us to classrooms. I lose sight of Kevin.

I like Mrs. Balou. She hugs me good-bye at the bus loading area. I look around for Kevin, but there are too many people. Children line up and confidently board buses. They all look the same to me, but a new classmate is getting on a bus and the driver looks familiar, so I follow her. Where is Kevin? The doors close and the bus pulls out in a wide arc.

We bounce along rural roads, dropping children at intervals, until there is only me. I don't feel very good about this. The driver cranes his neck to peer at me, but I stare out the window as if I don't notice. He pulls to the side of the road to ask my name, and radios the school office. We retrace the route back through town and out the other side until we reach my house. Stoic, I follow the driver to the front door, where he reassures my mother—who is worried about me and furious with my brother for not looking after me. I hold myself together until the bus pulls away, then burst into tears of relief.

"What are you crying for now?" my mother asks; her incredulous tone feels like an indictment. "You're home! You don't need to cry now!"

My mother didn't want to know about my anger, fear, or upset.

I didn't want her to know that I wasn't perfect.

"Hey, Jen. I learned the best song today. You've got to hear it!"

Jen says "You always say that. You're just going to sing 'Little Red Caboose.'"

"No, I'm not. Not this time. This is the latest song by the Beatles!"

"I don't believe you!" Jen stifles a giggle.

"You better believe it! You're going to love this song. I'll teach it to you," I wheedle.

We've been playing this game all week before falling asleep, tucked into matching twin beds under flowered bedspreads. Jen capitulates and asks me to sing it.

"Okay. This is the best song you'll ever hear!"

I take a deep breath and begin singing slowly and softly at first: "Little Red Caboose, chug, chug, chug, Little Red Caboose, chug, chug, chug . . . "

Jen joins me as we sing faster and louder. We climb out from under the covers and jump on our beds, laughing, singing, and whipping pillows at each other across the divide. Suddenly, with the acuity of eight years to my sister's five, I hear the creak of the stair rail and uneven footsteps ascending. I slip quickly beneath the covers, close my eyes, and force slow, regular breathing as the door opens.

"What are you doing jumping on the bed? I told you to be quiet and go to sleep."

I hunch my shoulders when I hear the smack.

"But Sara was doing it, too," Jen cries out.

"I don't want to hear another peep out of you."

With my back to Jen's tearstained cheeks, I craft my innocence. Betrayal is a sour taste in the back of my throat, soon forgotten.

My mother and I were both wed to my self-sufficiency and independence; my role in the family was unquestioned—it was all I knew. Being good was my foundation. No, not being good, being better—better than my brother for not angering my mother, better than my sister for not being needy or moody, for taking care of myself. And such goodness, I silently hoped, would bring a payoff. I'd get the attention that I wanted, though I didn't know what it was that I craved. Something good would come of being good, and that would be enough for me.

Some nights I can't get to sleep no matter how hard I try. The clock ticks monotonously on the top of my dresser, Jen's breathing is quiet and regular. I squeeze a tear from the corner of my eye and consider going downstairs. I mull it over and over before slowly putting my feet on the floor and beginning my laborious journey. I can usually get out the door all right. But I stop at the top of the stairs, willing my breath and my heartbeat to absolute silence, listening. Has Dad gone to bed? If so he's in the room right behind me. I can hear the TV in the living room. Maybe he's still up. The first step creaks. I step gingerly toward the outer edge; it creaks anyway. In fact, every step creaks. And my feet sound like sandpaper on the stairs no matter how quietly I place them. I wait. Can they hear me? Why can't I walk downstairs like a normal person? They're going to find out that I'm awake anyway! What's the matter with me?

Who am I afraid of?

I reach the hallway at the bottom of the stairs, where the cold wind sneaks under the big front door, swirls around my ankles and up my flannel nightgown.

Just walk out there. Just go.
The floor creaks.
"Is that you, Sara?" My mother.
I've been heard. I can walk into the living room now.
"Can't sleep?" My mother is unperturbed.

I nod to her and glance warily at my father, who grumbles, looks at his watch, and makes as if he's going to bed. What would he know about tossing and turning, this "asleep by the time his head hits the pillow, early to bed, early to rise" sleeper? Leave me to my mother, the "night owl, the just one more page, the 'it can't be morning yet'" sleeper.

She makes me hot chocolate and sits at the table while I drink it.

I think I will be able to sleep now. But it won't change anything. I'll creep again in a day or two, testing the weight of my body first on toe, then edge of foot, then heel, ready to retreat at the faintest groan of wood; my tears, my fears packed into one step, then the next. I will finally make it down the stairs, be discovered, drink the cocoa. I'll say, "I don't know," when she asks me why I can't sleep, and it will be true.

Catholic theologian Margaret Hebblethwaite writes in *Motherhood and God:*

> We are all made in the image of one mother and all have learnt from her, consciously or unconsciously, what it means to be gentle and caring, what it means to enfold and cherish, what it means to nourish and console. All comfort that comes from us, all creativity that breaks out from us, all tenderness that flows from us, comes ultimately from one source—our one, true and eternal mother, who is our God (Morehouse Group, 1994, 147).

My own mother was skeptical about this God. She didn't acknowledge my ache or understand my fear. Were her cups of cocoa and companionship enough to evoke that perfect love?

Chapter 3

Coming to Know

The morning after Mom's surgery, Jen and I return to the hospital after spending the night at Mom's town house for an uninterrupted night of sleep and a little psychological distance. When we arrive at Mom's room, she is groggy but petulant. "I was wondering when you two would get here."

Connie, even after a night of sleep in the hospital room, exudes her usual air of calm in the face of crisis. I remember it well from when Dad died.

I am not calm, though I may look so on the outside. The agitation I felt yesterday returns as I search for any indication that Mom has learned what was found during her surgery. I'm not sure what I'm so worried about. That she will explode? dissolve? freeze? That I won't know how to respond? That she'll be angry with us for not telling . . . for telling?

A nursing aide bustles into the room and distracts Mom with a bath and a change of bed linens. Connie, Jen, and I duck out for a quick powwow.

"What does she know? What has she asked?"

"Nothing," Connie replies. "She hasn't asked me anything, and the doctor hasn't been around yet this morning."

"I don't know how long I can stand this. I'm no good at lying."

The nursing aide passes us with a cheery greeting, and we head back into the room to fake it some more.

Later a nurse stops by to let us know the surgeon is on his way. "Good, now he'll tell her," I think.

We wait expectantly for the doctor to arrive, and are miffed when he asks us to leave the room so he can speak with Mom in private. We huddle at the end of the hallway and speculate on the conversation. Too soon, it seems, the surgeon opens the door, nods curtly in our direction, and strides away, leaving us with gaping mouths and unanswered questions.

"So, what did the doctor say?" we ask Mom, trying to sound casual. She looks at us as if we are crazy to be asking *her* for information.

"Well, he certainly wasn't very forthcoming," she complains.

I wish the doctor would at least tell her the rules of his game. She's holding the reins, and doesn't even know it.

"I need to go to the airport to meet Kevin's plane," Jen whispers to me. Though originally scheduled to arrive in three days, he booked a seat on the first available flight from San Francisco as soon as he heard from us. "Mom will be suspicious when she hears Kevin's coming early."

Mom glances our way. The morphine hasn't dulled her hearing—or her penchant for listening in on our conversations. "What's that about Kevin?" she asks.

"I'm going to pick him up at the airport. He decided he couldn't wait to come—he wants to be with us," Jen explains.

Mom is relieved to hear Kevin's on his way, and that the family will be together. If she wonders why he's coming early, she doesn't let on.

When Kevin arrives, Mom bursts into tears and strokes his face as he bends to kiss her. She gazes at her son, her little boy, her strong man. Despite their early struggles, my mother's relationship with my brother improved and deepened as he got older. She enjoys his sense of humor, his collection of friends, the music he introduces her to. When Dad died, Kevin was twenty-one and living a full life in Florida—with a girlfriend, a motorcycle, and a job as a roofer—but he suspended his independent pursuits for nearly a year to see Mom and Jen through the first terrible winter alone on the farm. After that he moved to San Francisco, and over the past nineteen years, has built a successful business as a carpenter and contractor, married, and had a daughter. Mom bemoans the fact that none of her children live nearby, but she loves traveling to San Francisco to spend time with Kevin, Tina, and four-year-old Teija. During Mom's Thanksgiving visit, they announced the impending arrival of another grandchild in early July.

Mom looks from Jen to Kevin to me as we gather around her bed. "You really do love me!" she announces with amazement and gratitude in her voice.

I nod and murmur an assent and pat her hand. But my face reddens as the naked intensity of her emotion evokes shame for the ways I've contributed to her feeling unloved over the years— failing to place the phone call, mail the card, or choose the gift in time for Mother's Day or her birthday. Withholding invitations, setting boundaries, keeping her out of my life though I knew she felt lonely, left out, and abandoned. Even as a young child, I knew how much she wanted affirmation, yet I rarely managed to squeak out an "I love you, Mommy," and then only with great effort.

"I come bearing gifts." Kevin's announcement pulls us through the moment. He hauls packages from his suitcase.

Tina has sent a perfumed body lotion called Beautiful, silver earrings shaped like coffee cups—a new twist on Mom's mug collection—framed photographs of Mom flanked by children, grandchildren, nieces, and nephews at last year's family reunion. Each gift affirms that Mom is beautiful, loved, and connected.

Looking at one of the family photos, I notice the T-shirt Mom was wearing during the family reunion. One of her favorites, it shows a cartoon sketch of a dead dog—a standing skeleton with a drooping tailbone—and the slogan, "In Dog Years, I'm Dead." I hated that ugly shirt with the morbid humor. Today it seems prophetic.

We spend the afternoon chatting and hanging about. Mom wafts in and out of the conversations, adding an opinion, a detail, or a sharp witticism before hitting the morphine-dosing button that gives her control over her pain medication without risk of overdose. The button becomes a forceful presence in the room; she spaces out each time she presses it.

At the end of the day, Mom knows no more about her condition than when it began.

I'm brimming with questions, however. During one of my trips to replenish Mom's ice supply, I find the chief surgical resident writing chart notes at the nurses' station, and ask if he's available to talk.

"I didn't assist at your mother's surgery," he explains, "but I've read through the notes. What would you like to know?"

He tears a blank sheet from a patient's chart and scribbles an anatomy lesson. "Your mother's tumor was located in the cecum, where the colon meets the large intestine. It grew outward, and slowly, which is why it produced no clear symptoms until it had grown large enough to begin to constrict the bowel. Unfortunately it has spread. There were small cancerous tumors sprinkled throughout the omentum, the wall of tissue that encloses the intestines, and there were several tumors in the liver. Some of those tumors and much of the omentum were removed during surgery. But not all."

"Somebody called it stage 4 cancer. What does that mean?"

The resident explains the systems used to describe the stages of cancer. The worst is 4 or D, and signifies that the cancer has metastasized to the liver. He tells me about survival rates, how doctors establish a prognosis, and the treatments available for stage 4 colon cancers.

"If my mother's going to die anyway, why did she have to suffer this surgery and the recovery process? Couldn't the doctor have done more tests in advance and spared her this experience?"

"Oh, there's no question that tumor had to come out. If it had been left to grow, your mother might have experienced a total bowel obstruction, which is immediately life threatening. I'm sorry."

I slip the diagrams and definitions into my pocket, feeling both comforted and subdued by all the information I've taken in.

When I return to Mom's room, she's talking with Nancy, her favorite nurse, the one who takes the time to sit and listen. Mom complains about the doctors not telling her much—she's fishing for information. Nancy deftly avoids the hints, making it clear that nurses don't trespass on doctors' turf.

The next morning, when the surgeon makes his daily visit, he doesn't kick me out of the room. Mom again asks him no questions. "An oncologist will stop by to see you later today," he states before leaving. Mom's face is expressionless; I can't tell if she's not listening, hasn't registered the implications, or is masking her reactions.

Early in the afternoon, a young doctor in a white lab coat embossed with the word *Oncology* slips into the room. Connie and I jump from our chairs and ease her out into the hall before Mom notices what's happening. Having been closed out of the information and decision-making loops by the surgeon, we are determined to find out why this doctor has come and what she intends to say.

"I'm going to talk to your mother about treatment options," she replies hesitantly. She seems cowed by our assertiveness.

"How can you discuss treatment options when my mother doesn't even know the findings from surgery?" I exclaim. "You should go slowly, and it would be better if we could all be in the room when you talk with her. My brother and sister just left for lunch. Can you come back later?"

Connie and I are relieved at her acquiescence, though not confident of her skill in talking with patients.

As the hour for the oncologist's return approaches, Connie and I try to prepare Mom for her visit by helping her articulate some questions.

"Mom, an oncologist is coming to see you in an hour," I say, touching her arm.

"Okay," she answers. With a click she presses the morphine-dosing button.

"What would you like to ask her?"

"Ask her? Well, I don't know. Maybe she . . ." Her voice trails off.

"Mom, maybe she what?" I ask.

"What?" Her eyes close, her mouth drifts open. We sit and wait.

Minutes pass. Mom's eyes flutter open, then widen. "What?" she says, taken aback by our attention; she moves her hand to the dosing device pinned to her chest.

"You were telling us what you'd like to ask the oncologist."

"I was?"

Click.

When the oncologist returns, the family is reassembled and ready. Except for Mom. She's groggy, hovering near oblivion. The oncologist begins cautiously, but after getting no response from Mom, barrels ahead with information she seems determined to impart. Connie and I interrupt now and then, asking questions clearly and loudly in an effort to capture Mom's attention, but she appears to have absented herself.

By late afternoon Mom is more alert. She knows her grandchildren will arrive from Philadelphia soon, and for the first time since the surgery, she is focusing on someone else's feelings. "What will the kids think of all these machines and tubes?" she worries. "Ring for the nurse. I want to be sitting in the chair when they come, not lying in bed. And Sara, please get them out of here quickly if I get too tired."

When Kenwyn, Justin, Phillip, and Kalila arrive, I head them off at the nurses' station and shepherd them into a waiting room. The children are energetic after six hours in the car; they test the chairs and couches and rifle through old *Highlights* magazines. I catch each in a hug and breathe deeply of child smells and life outside the hospital. They listen intently when I turn serious and describe what they will see in their grandma's hospital room—the IV pole and oxygen tubes, the monitors and machines. Kenwyn and I walk them down the hall to Mom's room.

"Wow, look at all the flowers!" Justin is the first to warm to the situation. He asks about the breathing gadget, and Mom asks if he and Phillip, eight-year-old twins, want to try it.

Five-year-old Kalila stays on my lap; she won't look at her Grandma Jane. When she scowls and ostentatiously holds her nose, complaining about the odor in the room, I whisk her out for a walk in the hall. When we return I hand her a stuffed bear that Mom received as a get-well wish, and distract her from all she finds to see, hear, or smell in the room.

I notice how alert Kenwyn and I are to the interaction between Mom and the children; we encourage conversation, add our own cheerful comments, and keep the mood light and comfortable. Together and alone we are good at this aspect of parenting, tapping into the needs of each child and tuning in to the shifting energies in their relationships. I watch Mom closely, and catch the quick look she gives me to signal that it's time for the visit to end. I can tell that she's pleased with how it went.

That night Kevin, Jen, and my family crowd into Mom's small town house. Justin and Phillip construct forts in the living room, draping sheets and blankets over furniture and lining their dens with piles of pillows and sleeping bags. Kalila finds a space under the stairs. "Can we sleep in our forts tonight?" they ask.

Jen finds one of her favorite Dr. Seuss books on a shelf and reads to Kalila. Justin and Phillip roughhouse with their Uncle Kevin. The house fills with irrepressible warmth, despite our anxiety and grief. I feel a pang of regret about how little time we've spent at Mom's house over the years, how we are creating, in her absence, the coziness and family togetherness she has always wished for.

The next day we alternate entertainment for the children with visits to the hospital. At a local college ice rink, I help the children lace their skates, hold Kalila's hand for several laps around the rink, then cut loose and race against a college kid in hockey skates, coming to a breathless stop in front of the children. "Wow, you can skate fast!" Justin says. I laugh because they don't realize that the young man was humoring me and that I almost fell on the turn; I was remembering what it felt like to fly at the end of a string of skaters in junior high school, playing crack-the-whip. For a moment I forget that my mother is dying.

Later Kenwyn takes the children to the planetarium, and I return to Mom's bedside. I am flooded again with anxiety about her state of knowing. When one of Mom's nurses stops me in the hall to ask how I'm coping, I admit I'm worried. "I'm sure the oncologist they've sent us is competent, but Mom needs someone who can tune in to her emotional state. She still doesn't know what the surgeon found when he cut her open!"

"I might be able to help," the nurse responds. "One of my best friends, a nurse on this unit, is battling breast cancer. She knows all the oncologists." We talk about the pros and cons of various doctors, and she encourages me to make a proactive choice.

By Monday morning Mom and I are on our own; Kenwyn and the children, Jen, Kevin, and Connie return to their homes and routines. I meet with a different oncologist, one recommended for his experience and bedside manner, and he agrees to see my mother that afternoon. In the interim I try to prepare Mom, telling her that the new oncologist is nice and easy to talk to, very experienced. She listens intently, even asks me a few questions. I think she is getting ready to know.

When the oncologist arrives, Mom reaches out and grabs my hand. Her eyes pool with tears, but do not spill, as she listens to the doctor say "spread to your liver" and "incurable." When he leaves I reach around the tubes and wires to hug Mom, and she grips me tightly.

"Why, just when I finally believe you kids love me, why do I have to lose that now?" she cries.

I listen and nod and cry, and sense that we are on sacred ground.

"I don't want to miss out on seeing my children grow older and my grandchildren grow up!"

I think of Justin, Phillip, Kalila, Teija, the new life growing within Tina, the yet-to-be fertilized eggs in Jen, and I ache for them. They are too young to realize what they will lose.

I think of myself. There will be no chance to make things better between us.

"My life may not seem exciting, but I like it!" Mom continues. "I like going out to dinner with my friends. I like reading books. I like going to the movies. I'm not ready to stop doing all those things!"

"Oh, Mom, thank you!" I say softly into her shoulder.

Instead of talking about the grief and anger in her life: polio, widowhood, aging, depression, disappointment, the distancing of her children—losses that often dominate the emotional space between us—she affirms what she loves about her life and mourns its passing.

Despite my fears that I won't know how to be with my mother as she comes to know she is dying, it turns out to be simple. All that is required of me is to be present to a divine moment, to listen and to love.

Chapter 4

Legacy of Caring

It is more peaceful and tender between Mom and me since the oncologist talked with us about the cancer. Life feels more precious when lived in the awareness of death. To be able to laugh and cry and share all sorts of feelings about living and dying seems to diminish the fear.

It occurs to me that if my father were still alive, my interactions with my mother would be different. Aside from suspecting that she might not have advanced cancer if Dad had been there to notice her deterioration sooner and urge a visit to the doctor, I think he, not me, would be the one to support and encourage her now. His absence creates the opportunity and the imperative for me to care so intimately for Mom. It seems strange to describe this as a pleasure and a privilege, but as I witness her physical, emotional, and spiritual pain, and as I reach out to comfort her and she is soothed, I embody compassion that is greater than me alone.

I learned many lessons in caring from my father, who was a consummate caregiver. A founding principle of my parent's marriage must have been my father's unspoken promise to enable my mother to live a life unhindered by handicap. Dad found a way around impediments Mom wouldn't think to challenge. He was alert to her disappointment and created opportunities she wouldn't imagine were open to her. He respected her preferences for manual gear shifts and multi-storied homes, even when they required more effort. He did all this with no sense of burdon. To my mother's continual surprise, her crutches and all they represented didn't faze my father.

"I saw a woman walking down the street who looked just like you," I once heard my father tell my mother. "I almost called out to her, but then she turned, and I saw that it wasn't you."

"Oh, was she walking with crutches?" Mom asked.

"No," Dad replied, with a confused shake of the head. "Why?"

Dad's passion for caring, saving, and protecting went far beyond Mom—he quit his job with the mining company, unable to tolerate how it demoralized its employees; he opened a gas station, and often stayed late to finish a repair or to help a traveler with a broken-down car; he moved the family back to his hometown of Sandy Creek to be available to his mother, younger brother, grandmother, and handicapped half brother after his father died. And he befriended a lonely old lady living on a long-fallow farm.

Daddy's eyes light up when he tells a story. It makes dinnertime fun.

"I was driving along the Center Road today when I noticed a large, weather-beaten farmhouse set back from the road, ringed by tall maple trees. I thought it was completely abandoned, but when I peeked through one of its soot-clouded windows, a pair of faded blue eyes in a wrinkled face peered back at me. I decided I'd better knock on the door and introduce myself properly! An old lady named Neva answered the door. She's lived in the old place for over fifty years. Her husband died twenty-five years ago, and they never had any children, so there hasn't been much happening there for quite some time.Why don't we all drive out there sometime!"

"I want to go!" I say.

There is no path through the tall grass to the front door at the farm, so Daddy leads us around to the back. Neva sees us coming. She shuffles outside, using a hoe for a cane, and wearing a faded cotton housedress printed with tiny flowers, a grimy-looking apron and an old black cardigan with holes in the elbows. She is happy to see Dad; he introduces us and tells us to lean in close and speak loudly because she is nearly deaf. I hold my breath when I yell into that big old ear under the scraggly dirty-gray hair.

She invites us to come inside through a dark woodshed, lit only by tiny streams of sunlight that shine through the cracks in the walls and ceiling, then into a large room with blackened walls and ceiling. "That black is creosote, residue from wood fires," Daddy tells us quietly, and points to the woodstove in the corner. I can see only the outlines of trees and outbuildings through the sooty windows. The only running water into the house dribbles into a yellowed enamel utility sink before draining into a large crock, half-filled with grease-slicked liquid. Neva's bed is next to the wall, a jumble of dingy sheets and torn quilts. There is one bare lightbulb hanging in the middle of the room, casting a dim glow.

"Come see the front parlor," Daddy encourages. He helps us notice the good stuff and ignore the bad. This room is the only one out of twelve that looks nice. There is a carved wooden pump organ against one wall. "Give it a try," Daddy suggests, and shows me how to pump vigorously with my feet. He pulls out the stops as I press the keys and play an eerie rendition of "Love Is Blue."

Leaving the house to visit the ramshackle sheds and huge barn, I suck fresh air deep into my lungs to clear the scent of age and decay. My father is delighted by possibility.

For several years Dad patched Neva's roof when it leaked, kept her wood box filled, and brought her a portion of our Sunday dinner every weekend. Jen and I sometimes tagged along to the farm, playing tea party with rusty scraps of metal from old farm tools, bright red berries from a bush by the barn, and puddles of rainwater; collecting bright autumn leaves; or building a snowman. I liked being with my father while he worked on his projects, though he didn't talk much. His love was a big warm hand helping, a deep belly laugh, a well-timed joke, a crinkly-eyed smile.

My mother quietly seethed in the partially demolished kitchen of our family home, resenting the time and energy my father spent at the farm even as she admired his kindness and zeal. She hid her anger from him, and didn't nag about the promised renovations or unfinished projects in her own house.

The complex web of my parents' relationship, woven of compassion and caring, dependency and disappointment, promises and secrets, entangled me without my awareness. Like a fish that realizes its home is the water only after sailing above its surface in pursuit of a dragonfly, I gained insight into the nature of our family and my role in it by leaving.

My new dress feels silky as I straighten the skirt over my knees. I am on a jet, descending toward the Syracuse Airport, with butterflies in my stomach. It is five weeks since I flew to Chicago to visit my Grandma and Grandpa Klein; I've turned ten since then.

I've never owned a dress this fancy. It has long, white cuffs that stretch from my wrist to my elbow, with five pearl buttons, and puffy sleeves above that. Grandma and I have talked about my dress a lot since she bought it for me. I like these words: cotton sateen, dropped waist, Peter Pan collar. I lift my chin higher and seek my reflection among the clouds in the tiny airplane window.

The plane lands, and the stewardess helps me through the crowd to the gate. Out of the corner of my eye, I catch a glimpse of my mother and father and sister waving from the barrier. My brother must be hanging out with his friends. I don't look at them straightaway. I don't want them to think I am homesick or anything. "We missed you!" they say when we meet. I smile what I think to be a sophisticated closed-lip smile.

Daddy hugs me; then, holding me by the shoulders, pushes me to arms' length and examines my dress.

"Wow!"

"You look lovely, Sweetie," my mother interjects.

I am self-conscious. I jump into the story of the dress so they'll stop looking at me as if I've changed. I hope they notice that I've changed.

"Grandma and I took the train from Waukegan to Chicago to go to Marshall Field's," I begin.

I decide not to tell them how I inhaled the perfume on the ground floor of the department store while gazing up at the elegant chandeliers and avoiding the ladies with the infusers, or how my stomach rose slightly before thumping back down when the elevator man braked for the fourth-floor young ladies' department. I don't say how my fingertips delighted in the feel of satin and velvet as I followed the store clerk into the fitting room, stepped out of my Sears-catalog shorts set, raised my hands so Grandma could slip the dress over my head, held my hair while she zipped and buttoned, and turning, caught my image in the mirror, a new girl. Over the shoulder of this new girl in the fancy dress, my grandmother smiled with pleasure and an urgency to indulge. The price tag dangling from the long, white cuff was stamped $25.00. There was no yellow clearance tag.

I don't mention that I let my hips sway as we passed through the revolving door and onto the street, me clutching the shopping bag filled with the dress and a pair of black shoes with small but definite heels, Grandma's high heels clicking on the sidewalk beside me. I only resume the story at the moment when I felt something plop on my head and instinctively reached my hand to see what it was, and Grandma said, "Stop, don't touch it," and whipped out her white, lace-trimmed handkerchief to wipe it away.

"A pigeon pooped on my head outside of Marshall Field's!" I announce to my parents and sister with combined horror and glee, abandoning the air of maturity and restraint.

"Eeeu!" shouts my sister.

My father puts his arm around my shoulder in a confidential manner. "That reminds me of a little story," he begins.

The story is long and detailed and involves a bird named Foo.

Oh, this is a joke, not a story; I should have seen the punch line bearing down on us.

"If the Foo s✳✳✳s, wear it!" Daddy says loudly as he reaches the finale.

I giggle, both embarrassed and flattered to be considered old enough to hear a joke with the s-word in it.

We walk toward the airport exit. Unlike my grandmother's clicking high heels, my mother's soft-soled flats and rubber-tipped crutches are quiet on the linoleum, except for an occasional squeak. Daddy is carrying my suitcase. I carry Mommy's purse.

Five weeks with my long-distance grandparents has changed me; I traveled alone, held my own in unfamiliar places, and forgot the color of my bedspread. My grandmother indulged me with apple fritters and Swedish pancakes, introduced me to my Illinois relatives, bought me a snazzy new dress and shoes, wiped my head clean when the pigeon struck, and required no special sensitivity from me. I have matured, but at the same time I feel more secure in my youngness; I'm still just a girl.

Home again. I grip the smooth leather handles of my mother's purse and notice its weight.

The summer I turned eleven, my father was offered the job of business manager for the school district of Geneva, New York, and by September he was driving ninety miles between Sandy Creek and Geneva on Sundays and Fridays to assume his new responsibilities and find us a new house. On weekends he regaled us with impersonations of his eccentric landlady and tales of our new town; we were caught up in his infectious enthusiasm and couldn't wait to move.

I entered my Geneva school after Christmas. My first lessons in being the new girl were learned on the playground, thanks to a gang of taunting, teasing girls who surrounded me at recess and after school to provoke me to fight. I discovered that I was a pacifist; it was easier to drop my arms to my sides and turn away, hiding my nervous amusement at the lame insults and forced sneers of my attackers. I slowly cultivated friendships among the quiet sympathizers who watched from the sidelines.

Despite this uncomfortable initiation to my new social world, I came into my own over the next few years. I played flute in the marching and concert bands, made a lively though unsuccessful bid for student council president, and excelled academically. I led my classmates in antics to annoy our fun-loving social studies teacher, developed crushes, fended off the crushes of others, and met my friends at the local strip mall to spend babysitting money.

My mother, an urbanite, was happy about the move to Geneva. The town was fifteen times the size of Sandy Creek, was home to an excellent liberal arts college, and offered cultural and political diversity. She found a volunteer position with a local Head Start program, which led to a part-time job as office manager of a day-care center. She developed strong friendships. The house in Geneva was more compact and easier to get around in and maintain than the last. She spent every Saturday baking all our bread for the coming week.

I was fully ensconced in my position as the good child, the easy one in the family. While my sister got yelled at for her messy room, or for spending more time staring in the bathroom mirror rehearsing commercials for cleaning products than cleaning it, or for not practicing the piano, I kept my room neat, volunteered for household chores, and avoided conflict. Kevin was in high school, and seemed to stay out of the dynamics of favoritism, keeping busy with wrestling or the school play and hanging out with friends in the local park or in black-lit, psychedelically painted basement rec rooms.

But despite my investment in the favored position, I kept my emotional distance. My mother ascribed this to my personality, seeing me as stubborn, aloof, and independent. But I sensed a certain danger in getting too close.

I rush through the door, throwing my schoolbooks to the ground as I race for the bathroom. No matter how often I make this desperate dash at the

*end of my mile-long walk home from school in the afternoon, I never seem
to remember to use the bathroom at school before I leave. My mother
shakes her head at me when I come out of the bathroom. She doesn't have
to say anything; I've heard it without heeding it before.*

*"I got an essay back in English today," I hand it to Mom. I got an A
and "Good work!" written at the top.*

*Mom begins to read, stopping several times to point out misspelled
words and grammatical mistakes.*

*She always finds mistakes with how I say things and never comments
on what I say. I hate that! I'm not going to show her my work anymore.*

*I'm not going to tell her about my boyfriend either. His friends call
him Jimmer. He's twelve or thirteen, and has blonde hair. I think he goes
to the Catholic school because I've never seen him at my junior high.
He's not really smart or funny, but he's cute, and my friend told me to
say I liked him because she likes his friend. We saw Jimmer and his
friends riding their bikes, and he showed me his house. It's huge, on a
block with big yards.*

*I race to answer the phone whenever it rings. I lie when Mom asks who
is calling. I tell her it's my friend Julie.*

*Then after two weeks, she overhears my conversation. "Hello. Oh.
Okay. Good-bye."*

"Who was that?" Mom asks.

"It was Jimmer calling to break up with me."

"Who's Jimmer? I didn't even know you had a boyfriend!"

I shrug.

*For a week I overhear Mom telling her friends how I got this break-
up call, and she didn't even know I had a boyfriend.*

*Maybe some girls talk to their mothers about boys, but not me. I don't
like her asking me things or blabbing it around to everyone. It feels like
she's stealing my feelings.*

After moving to Geneva, we remained connected to Sandy
Creek, going there most summer weekends to visit my grand-
mothers and to camp at the farm, where we slept in tents, cooked

and ate at picnic tables in the barn, and collected water from the spring. Neva died soon after we left Sandy Creek, and bequeathed her estate to my father: a one-hundred-year-old farmhouse on 250 acres of land, with a beaver pond, a stand of towering hardwood trees, rolling fields overgrown with sumac and blackberry bushes, a winding spring-fed stream that emptied into big Sandy Creek, a large barn and outbuildings, and an odd assortment of well-worn antiques, which brought almost enough at auction to pay the back taxes included in the inheritance.

My father loved working around the farm, finding endless chores, while my mother sat at the picnic table where the sun streamed into the barn, reading, working crossword puzzles, or preparing meals. I sometimes brought a friend to tramp through the woods, wade in the stream, brave the mud and leeches for a swim in the beaver pond, or balance on a beam in the barn to grab a rope and swing out over piles of ancient hay rotting in the hold. Dad bought an old VW Beetle for fifty dollars, and taught us to drive on dirt tracks around the fields. We practiced on our own until Kevin, breaking the unofficial speed limit for a curvy stretch of trail, crashed into the outhouse, knocked it off its base, and stalled on the railroad tie supporting it, one wheel of the Beetle still spinning over the muck-filled hole in the ground. Though it was empty, at the moment of impact we couldn't help imagining people flying off the seats and into the trees, had it been doubly occupied.

Friends and family often joined us at the farm. Dad captured people's imagination with his energy and enthusiasm, and they gathered for the equivalent of an Amish barn raising to clear a roadway into the woods or plant pine trees or clean out the barn. One year the men helped my father dismantle a historic foundry that was slated for demolition in a nearby town, hauling huge, rusted iron machinery, tools, and materials to a back field at the farm. The men arrived eager to roll up their sleeves and sweat, the women to prepare salads and casseroles and chat and laugh with my mother, the children to tramp through the woods. At night we sat around a campfire, singing, talking, and looking at the stars.

Dad woke us at two o'clock in the morning one time to watch the northern lights flicker and dance in the star-studded sky.

There was tension between my parents about the time we spent at the farm. My mother worried about my father's ulcers and high blood pressure, and thought he worked too hard both on the job and at the farm. Perhaps in connection with that, we began a tradition of getting away from it all for a three-week camping trip on Deer Isle, Maine. We went clamming, swimming, and fishing, drove along the rocky coastline to visit quaint fishing villages, or watched Arno Day and his son build wooden lobster boats in their big construction barn on the edge of Long Cove.

Although my father tried to escape the demands and unwind from the stress of his school district job—a set of responsibilities that would be divided into three full-time jobs after he resigned—someone from his office always managed to track him down with an urgent problem. One day Dad dropped in to Arno's barn to check on the progress of a boat that was nearly ready for launching and to shake his mind free of a phone call from a colleague. Arno moved a plane rhythmically along the surface of a long board until it was smooth, and Dad instinctively stepped forward to help as he passed it up to his son to nail it in place. An idea began to percolate.

Back in Geneva at the start of the school year, Dad's proposal to the board that they hire a separate negotiator to handle disputes between teachers and the administration—a move that would relieve some of the pressure in his job—was turned down again. Then the cardiac specialist, concerned about his high blood pressure and a suspicious heart murmur, recommended that he lower his stress level. Dad wrote a letter to Arno Day, offering his services as an apprentice boat builder. The small house on the campground was available for rent. Arno accepted Dad's offer, to the tune of $2.75 an hour. Dad requested a leave of absence from his Geneva job, and we moved to Deer Isle in November. I was a junior in high school, Jen was in the seventh grade, and Kevin was away at college.

Leaving a college town that was near several major cities for an isolated and provincial island off the coast of Maine was to involve more losses than I could realize at the time. I took for granted the intellectual stimulation of my teachers and classmates and the range of opportunities in music and sports that were available to me in Geneva, and was caught up in Dad's incurable optimism, his restless need for change, and the radical appeal of having a father drop out of the rat race. Instead of mourning, I readjusted my expectations of school, made a friend or two, found a Japanese musician living in a nearby Buddhist colony with whom to continue my flute lessons, and warmed the bench on the basketball team. With the temporary shrinking of our horizons, Mom, Dad, Jen, and I enjoyed a new kind of closeness. Dad worked a few hundred yards from the house, lunched at home, and enjoyed it when we dropped in on him after school. Jen and I slept in the same room, and talked more than we had for years. Events in Deer Isle tended to be multigenerational, so we went as a family to school dances, basketball games, and church suppers. Friends and family from Geneva and Sandy Creek visited us on the island, eager to share in our Maine adventure.

Strain between my parents became more visible.

"Mom," I call out, storming into the house and bursting into tears all at once, "my canoe paddle is all messed up! Dad's been working on it! It's not his!"

I brought my wood-shop project home from school on Friday so I could put in more time on it. It's supposed to be finished next week, and I don't get enough class time to work on it. I'm pretty slow, shaving off each slice of wood slowly and carefully so it always looks smooth.

I can't believe Dad worked on it without asking me. He really tore into it, shaving off a huge section, roughing up the surface. I don't care if it's the way it should be done. I wanted to do it my way.

"Don't ask me to talk to him, Sara," Mom's tone of voice revealing an anger and frustration with Dad that I didn't know she felt. "I'm

tired of being the one to point out what he does that upsets others. If you want him to know how you feel, you tell him. He needs to know that I'm not the only one who gets upset at him when he does something like this."

After a few months of living in Maine, a yearning for what I'd lost edged out the appeal of newness and change. With the spring school holiday approaching, I proposed a trip back to Geneva to visit friends. Mom and Jen were eager to go, but Dad said he needed to stay and continue working. "I could do most of the driving," I suggested, suspecting it would be too much for Mom alone. "It'll give me practice for my driver's test." The decision was made, and Jen and I called our friends to line up places to stay for the ten-day vacation.

In the next week, however, there were hushed conversations between Mom and Dad, calls to his doctor in Geneva, discussions of angina—hardening of the arteries—and the scheduling of an appointment. Dad would come to Geneva after all.

I was disappointed, selfishly. My father wouldn't relinquish the driver's seat on such a long haul, and I'd been looking forward to the experience of independence in organizing the trip, charting our route, and driving across four states on my learner's permit.

I can't believe Dad let me be in charge of this trip! He's been sitting in the back seat, reading or looking out the window, since we left Deer Isle. He didn't even bark instructions or warnings while I drove through Boston's rush hour, clinging to the edge of the road and hovering under the speed limit. I giggle every time I catch sight of him in the rearview mirror.

When we arrived in Geneva, we split up to stay with different friends. Dad had an appointment to see his doctor; they discovered life-threatening hardening of his arteries, and scheduled him for open-heart surgery to replace two of the valves leading to his heart with veins from his leg.

Our planned reunion with old friends had become a major family crisis.

While Dad had his chest cut open, his ribs stretched apart, his heart rearranged, then stiched up again, Mom hovered at the hospital, panicked, petrified of losing him, and trying to convince herself that her world was not coming to an end. Ninety miles away in Geneva, Jen contracted infectious mononucleosis, and lay day after day in the spare bed in her friend's room, staring listlessly out the window as the trees launched their first leaves, feeling lonely and alone, pining for her mother and fearing for her father. I suffered the least. I stayed with a good friend, resumed the school schedule I'd abandoned in November, went to the prom with the boyfriend I'd left behind, and believed the zipperlike scar running the length of my strong, invulnerable father's chest signified a bad problem fixed for good.

After three weeks Dad was discharged from the hospital, and Mom's anxiety eased enough for her to notice the needs of her daughters and make plans to return to Maine. Dad would stay behind with his mother and grandmother for several weeks to attend follow-up medical appointments and heal more before traveling.

We decided I should get my driver's license before we made the trip back to Maine—my learner's permit didn't authorize me to drive outside of New York State, so I'd already made one illegal journey. Friends filled me up with stories of people who failed the driving test and examiners who were biased against women. "Wear a miniskirt," one advised. "That will sway the examiner in your favor." I don't know if it was the stretch of thigh I revealed or my perfect K-turn, but I was relieved to pass on my first try.

I drove my mother and sister back to Maine in the pouring rain.

Chapter 5
Vulnerability

It feels as if Mom and I have been floating above the anguish and hopelessness evoked by a diagnosis of terminal cancer, buoyed by emotional connection, tender acceptance, and love. But recently her mood is clouding and becoming heavy. I feel myself sinking, too, into the physical reality, dragged down by the pragmatism that surrounds us. Hospital staff cycle relentlessly through Mom's room, asking with false cheerfulness: "Are her lungs clear? Is she mobilizing? How's the gastrointestinal system working? Is the wound healing?"

Mom is annoyed with the poking and prodding and the demands that she sit, move from bed to chair, walk, breathe deeply. She whimpers to me when we're alone: "I'm tired and weak. Can't they let me rest?" But too many people are pressuring her to perform daring acts of recovery. She can't escape.

Except in humor. Always a master of one-liners, Mom hasn't lost her sense of timing.

One day, a nurse pokes her head around the doorway with a cheerful hello, then turns to drag a big, black machine into Mom's room. "I just need to set you up with this. It'll only take a minute." Mom and I catch each other's eye as we scan the crowded room, wondering how the nurse will find space and an electrical outlet with the furniture and medical equipment already crowding the room. She maneuvers between the chair and the couch, pulls the machine behind her, leans over and stretches to plug the cord into an empty outlet. She turns with a satisfied smile, and then laughs to find herself trapped in the corner.

"Hand me that plastic spoon on my tray," Mom says with a deadpan expression. "I'll tunnel a passageway into the next room for you."

Avoidance, denial, humor—we used those same familiar methods to beat back the sense of vulnerability and apprehension that Dad's open-heart surgery introduced into our family. During the eight weeks that Dad stayed behind in New York to heal and attend follow-up medical visits, Mom, Jen, and I relegated fear to a subliminal undercurrent and put a positive spin on his health crisis: "Everything will be fine . . . Lucky to catch the problem when he did . . . Hooray for the wonders of modern medicine." We asserted normalcy with determination.

The day we got back to Maine, I discovered that the school's concert band was performing that evening. Unconcerned about missing three weeks of rehearsals and driving eight hours that day, I showed up to claim my chair as second flute. A few days later, Jen and I had dates to the school prom, which was, in this small town, a multigenerational event at which parents and grandparents watched from the bleachers, served punch, and danced along with the teenagers. Friends convinced Mom to come, too. I made a floor-length pink skirt, and wore it with a tank top and a sheer white blouse with ruffled collar and embroidered rosebuds. I was delighted with this find from the back corner of Mom's dresser drawer, but she laughed at me, unable to see it for anything other than the top to Grandma Klein's old pajamas. Still, she bragged later that Jen and I were the prettiest girls at the prom.

I decided to surprise Dad, and began planting the garden he had planned for the spring, envisioning little green shoots poking through the ground by his return. It hadn't seemed like much of a plot when he staked it out, but as I began to turn the ground and dig, it grew bigger and bigger. I puzzled over the backs of the seed packets. How many to a hole? How far apart? After a few brief attempts at gardening, I threw my hoe in the corner of the barn and wiped angrily at the tears on my mud-stained cheeks.

I missed Dad, not just because he wasn't home but because I could no longer think of him as invincible.

But then he came home and was his same old self, although thinner and weaker. Joking and cheerful, he assured us that he was recovering well, and banished our worries.

When school ended I found a summer job as a waitress at a local lobster restaurant—a dollar an hour plus tips. In my new white uniform, black apron, sensible shoes, and lobster-shaped earrings, I arrived fresh and eager for my first day on the job. Some people know instinctively how to wait tables. Others eat out enough to know what makes for a good waitress. Some restaurants train new staff. At The Lobster Pool, I was handed an order pad, assigned to a section of tables, and thrown to the customers. Feeling lucky if I managed to deliver the right meal to the right person that first night, the thought of bussing my tables never crossed my mind. Plates piled high with lobsters displaced empty salad bowls; then, littered with shells and plastic bibs, they were shoved aside to make way for pie plates and coffee mugs, until at the end of the meal there was no room on the table for my tip.

I figured out a few things about waitressing as the summer dragged on, and was occasionally rewarded with a tip that brought my hourly wage up to the federal minimum, but the job was a sobering confrontation to my self-confidence and my faith in the generosity of others.

Meanwhile, our year in Maine was coming to an end. One night my parents announced our next move. We would not return to Geneva. Dad would resign his job with the school district, and we'd live on the Sandy Creek farm. He could slow down, start anew, and work the land. I would return to the school I'd attended in grades K-6 to finish high school.

I didn't think to complain or protest, tuned in as I was to my family's sense of vulnerability. However, when a brochure arrived from the University of Rochester inviting me to apply for early admission, I was excited by the prospect of beginning college early, in January of my senior year of high school. I submitted an application, energized by the idea of creating my own plan rather than simply responding to family circumstances.

In late August we loaded a U-Haul truck with our furniture and moved to the Sandy Creek farmhouse. It was as Neva had left it: cold and drafty, soot-blackened and grimy, rank with the odor of abandoned mouse nests, bat droppings, mildew, and creosote. We cleared away rubble in the more promising bedrooms, found a space for the piano, organized a living room in the old front parlor with the faded gilt wallpaper and the Franklin woodstove, and installed a toilet, which we flushed by pouring a bucket of water down the bowl until the plumbing was updated. While Dad worked to create a functional bathroom and kitchen, and to install a convertible wood-to-oil-burning furnace, we slept at the farm, rode the bus to school each day, and visited Grandma Corse's apartment for an occasional dinner and shower. By mid-October we were able to live at the farm full-time.

In my first days back at school, I felt like Rip Van Winkle, as surprised by what hadn't changed in the six years since I'd moved away as I was by what was different; for some reason I expected no one to recognize or remember me. Some of my friends from the elementary years had moved, gone to private school, or left for college. I hadn't stayed in touch with anyone beyond the first year away from Sandy Creek, and my efforts to reconnect with classmates were hampered by the persistence of outdated memories. Instead of a high school senior, I saw a five-year-old whose noisy sobbing in the waiting line for vaccinations had set my own lip quivering in fear, or an eight-year-old who, afraid to ask our stern gym teacher for a bathroom pass, froze in embarrassment as a dark stain spread across the front of his trousers and a puddle grew on the floor at his feet. But before long I had a new group of friends to joke with in study hall, a boyfriend to watch on the basketball court and be silly with in the hallways, the position of first flute in the concert band, a place on the volleyball team, and top rankings as a student.

I went to the University of Rochester for an interview and a tour, and was attracted by all that I saw. But by the time my acceptance letter arrived, I was fully engaged in my final year of high school, and decided that another change was more than I needed. I deferred admission from January to September, and my college search was over after one application.

Although it was more rustic than most families would tolerate, I enjoyed our new lifestyle in the country. After school and on weekends, I helped Dad cut firewood, load logs onto the wagon pulled behind an old John Deere bulldozer, and split and stack wood into cords to dry for use the following year. We repaired the old chicken coop, and when the chicks arrived in cardboard boxes, I nurtured the yellow balls of fluff that pecked at the grain and scurried around on twig-legs. Once they began to lay, each day held promise of an Easter egg hunt.

Acclimatization to things physical or emotional is often an imperceptible process. Winters are harsh in northern New York State, and icy winds blew snow and bitter cold across Lake Ontario to our home in Tug Hill country. In my large, second-story corner bedroom, windows rattled loosely in their casings with the wind. When I climbed into bed each night, it took five minutes of shivering under four blankets and a sleeping bag to create a pocket of warmth sufficient to last until morning. My father jumped out of his cozy marital cocoon at dawn, shoved feet into icy slippers, and loaded the stove with wood before the last embers went cold. I wouldn't know until the next winter, after four months in an overheated college dormitory rendered me incapable of warming my bed without the help of a heated soapstone, a fifth blanket, and a hat, just how much adaptation I had made that year.

As winter gave way to early spring, I checked the sap buckets hanging from the maple trees when the school bus dropped me off at the end of my driveway each afternoon, and when we'd collected enough, I stirred the vat of faintly sweet liquid until it boiled down to thick amber syrup. Dad and I gave gardening a second chance that spring, planting corn, staking the pea plants and tomatoes, weeding between the rows of beans, and slapping at the black flies that attacked in June. By August we were plucking crispy new carrots from the earth and telling Mom to put the water on to boil—sweet corn tastes best when the time from field to table is five minutes or less.

At the end of the summer, I was ready to leave our rough but comfortable living conditions at the farm for my new home at the University of Rochester. My parents helped me move into my dorm room, make my bed, and unpack my clothes. We chatted with my new roommate and her parents, but I was soon itching to respond to the call of Fleetwood Mac blasting from a huge stereo system erected in the quad for freshman orientation. Dry-eyed and impatient, I hugged my tearful mother and my father good-bye and didn't look back to wave as they drove out of the parking lot.

My first semester was a whirlwind of challenges as I adjusted to the academic demands of required freshman calculus, English literature, a foreign language, and the first course in my chosen major, Introduction to Psychology. I lived in one of the university's first coed halls, and my dorm mates and I became a tight-knit group. I learned my way around campus, downtown to the Eastman School of Music where I took flute lessons, and to an impoverished section of the city to tutor children in reading. Still, I felt intimidated by the city and campus; overwhelmed by the intellectual intensity, affluence, and life experience of my classmates; and distressed by the large lecture format of many classes and the competitiveness of fellow students. I worried that I'd been shortsighted and foolish to apply to only one school without considering other options. When an unsolicited brochure came in the mail from Kirkland College, I was attracted to this small liberal arts college for women with its seminars and alternative grading.

I shared my transfer dilemma with my parents at Christmas. I'd rarely talked about such problems with my father. He could be irritable after a stressful day, silent in a way that sometimes made me uncomfortable, and I tended to be afraid to approach him.

But as I told him about my doubts, I realized that a shift was taking place in our relationship: my father was beginning to relate to me as a young adult rather than as a child. He advised me to stay at the University of Rochester through my growing pains. He told me the story of his numerous college transfers. He was becoming a real person to me.

If I was going through some aching and groaning that fall, so was the family. My sister's boyfriend had died in a car accident at the end of the summer; she was grieving, angry at Mom and Dad's response, and struggling to keep her focus at school. My parents were struggling to survive on two part-time salaries—Mom's at the town library and Dad's with the Tug Hill Planning Commission—and to continue to make the farm more livable as winter approached. "We miss your sunshine," Mom said to me during the vacation. "When you come into a room, it's like a light goes on." The big, black room at the farm, so named because it caught and held the smoke and soot from Neva's woodstove for many years, wasn't the only gloomy thing in the house that season.

I returned to college in mid-January, comfortable with my decision to stay at the University of Rochester and eager to make the most of my second semester. I quickly forgot about the family woes back home.

"Connie will be here in an hour. You'd better get up!" I chide my sister. She's taken over my roommate's bed to experience a few days of college life. We stayed awake too late last night, talking and giggling. We wonder about Dad, who's been in the hospital since Monday afternoon, when he came home gray-faced after helping a friend move cuts of meat into his smokehouse and suggested Mom drive him to Watertown. The doctors at the hospital think it's his stomach.

"Where are we going for lunch?" I ask as Connie pulls out of the parking space and into the traffic streaming past the campus.

"Well, first we're stopping at the home of one of my friends. She lives nearby and is at work, so we'll have the house to ourselves."

As we drive we chat about the classes I'm taking this semester, Connie's new job, and the late January snowstorm that's threatening northern New York.

When do I notice the change in Connie's demeanor? Is it when she turns the key in the lock, pushes open the front door, and I sense the emptiness of the house, and suddenly wonder, Why are we here? Is it when she gestures toward the couch and asks us to sit? I know I was unsuspecting before then.

"Late last night," she begins, "your father had a massive heart attack, and he did not survive."

This sentence is too complex for me. It takes a moment to deconstruct it and find the troubling phrase. "He did not survive." What does Connie mean? Does she mean my father's dead?

I don't ask for clarification—I know by the sound of my screaming, intertwining with Jen's, what her answer would be.

For a few minutes there are no words—Jen and I wail and sob and writhe on the floor, as if to rub this truth away, as if to rub it in.

There is a moment of clarity in the swirling fog of grief and shock, and I speak for the first time. "Poor Mom! What will she do without Dad?"

Connie drives us home; it is a soggy Kleenex, stuffed-up nose, slippery road trip to Sandy Creek as it begins to snow more heavily.

The farmhouse fills with close friends who arrive before the roads get bad, and wait for the blizzard to stop, the roads to be cleared, and the family to come back to earth. We sit a weather-induced shiva for my father. The household reels with unruly emotions, twisting and turning from disbelief to acceptance, anger to grief, hilarity to lamentation, and back again. I console and am comforted. Meals appear and are eaten. I weep and sleep and dream and wake to realize that no nightmare could pale this reality. One of my father's friends, Garrie Stevens, a Methodist minister, writes a poem to capture these crazy snowbound days:

> Winter wind plays his nervous tunes
> On the curling clapboards
> And chases the sun low across her sky.
> While inside,
> Pictures pass around the big table

And across the wall—
But fail to draw him back.
In the church,
Songs and tears, poems and smiles,
Coffee, tea and love—
And he is still going away.
Dance of death
Upstairs, madness down.
One day leaks its sad silliness
Into the next, and every appointment
With reason is postponed.
Yet the snuggling
Mind heals itself—a little—enough
To keep the roof up, the smoke down,
The water in and the cold out.
And why isn't that
Enough?
Tomorrow will bring its own
Wounds and its own grace,
Because the dream was not his to own.
He belonged, as do we all.

"Dance of death upstairs, madness down." I hate Garrie's poem. How could my father be dancing in death? Why are we laughing? But I ask him to read it again and again; I love his poem. Could my father be dancing?

The friends who stay with us quietly note the family's needs—the critical renovations that are needed to enable Mom to live at the farm without Dad, how much care she must take to cross the uneven floor of the woodshed and the packed snow and patches of ice on the path to the car to scrape away the encrusted snow on the windshield and drive into town for bread and milk, how much wood is loaded into the stove to heat the house for a week. They promise to return in the summer for a work week-end in honor of Dad, to help make the place more livable.

We hold a funeral with family participation; many people can't attend because of the snow. Jen reads a poem she has written. I play a movement from a Mozart flute sonata; my mouth goes dry and my lips tremble. *We wear brightly colored clothing and talk about celebrating a life, not mourning a death. I wonder how it feels to be my great-grandmother and lose a grandson, to be my grandmother and lose a son, to be my mother and lose a husband. I consider their losses far more tragic than mine.*

My mother refuses to see Dad's body. It is moved directly from the hospital to the crematorium in Watertown. Mom tells us nothing about these arrangements; she doesn't call about collecting the ashes. "It's what I thought you all would want," she later defends her avoidance, her silence.

The house empties slowly over the next ten days, and when someone suggests that it's time for me to return to college, I consent, though the thought hasn't crossed my mind. What is a girl supposed to do after her father dies?

I take the green-and-red-plaid flannel shirt I gave my father for Christmas back to school with me. He never got around to wearing it; a line of white tailor's chalk is visible on the inside of the collar, and it doesn't smell like him.

At college my grieving is relegated to pauses between classes and schoolwork, late nights and weekends when my high school boyfriend visits from the college he's attending. He is tall and kind; his father died when he was twelve, and he can encircle my grief. I discover that I now belong to a secret club; its other members reveal themselves with the story of a mother or a father. "How did they die?" I ask, "How old were you?" We crack morbid jokes about dead parents; we aren't afraid of sadness.

But each time I go home, I discover how far behind the rest of the family I am in coming to terms with Dad's death. At university I have few reminders that he is gone; at the farm, everywhere I look is someplace he should be. Like our dog, who is still waiting patiently, mournfully, and without reward for the return of his master, I imagine my father alive. One day I'll climb onto a bus, maybe in Southern California, and look up at the driver, and there he will be.

How can my father be nowhere?

I am warned before my first visit home that a well-meaning but inexperienced friend "helped out" by cutting down the large beech tree that stood alone near the garden and chopping it up for firewood. But nothing could have prepared me to see the mangled branches and empty stump of this tall, full-canopied tree felled in its prime, too green to burn, under which my father and I had stood to escape the summer sun while planting or weeding. The loss of that tree is more acute, a greater affront, easier to rage against than the loss of my father.

I want to catch up with Jen and Kevin and Mom in the grieving process, but there's no going back for them, and I can't unpack the feelings I tuck away while at college. "I really miss Dad," I venture from time to time, having rolled the feeling around and around before getting up the nerve to share it. I want my mother to wonder what I'm thinking and to ask; I want to tell her so I can know myself. I want to cry and be comforted.

But my mother's response is always the same. "I miss him, too," she says, bursting into tears. In that instant my attention turns from my pain to hers; I become comforter. I generate the sunshine she counts on me to provide.

As Mom's pessimism, neediness, and bitterness, no longer contained by my father's steady presence or balanced by his optimism, grow desperate, grasping tentacles, I am caught in their grip. Though I try to stay out of reach or counter her pain with trumped-up displays of my own troubles, my efforts are without conviction and easily thwarted.

Yet when my visit is over, I am free to return to my independent life, escaping the emotional minefield of my family home. If I fill the empty spaces left by my father, it is only for a while, and then I'm gone.

At the end of my freshman year, I move home for the summer, anticipating that I will have time and support to get used to Dad's death. My grief is still fresh and raw; it swells as I wander the trails along the stream to the hardwood trees, past the stand of pines and the blackberry bushes, or out beyond the empty chicken coop, the stump of the murdered beech tree, and around the perimeter of the garden plot. There is no shortage of trees to witness my sobbing, but no one else wants to hear. I don't know how to fight for a place for my sadness, so I slip into the family mode of survival without stirring the waters. I take on my share of holding Mom's hand while she cries, and keep my feelings to myself.

I find work as a teacher's aide in a day camp for children with autism—a better job for me than waiting tables at The Lobster Pool. I commute twenty miles each way, along winding two-lane rural roads in our VW camper van. One rainy morning I enter a curve with too much speed, turning the steering wheel too far to avoid an approaching car. The top-heavy van skids and sways and rolls onto its side in the ditch while I bounce around inside. Aside from a dent in the van, a bruise on my shoulder, and the cost of a tow truck, no harm is done. Still, I'm shaken. Mom offers her usual response, "Don't tell me; I don't want to know." A few days later, a visiting relative offers me fatherly words of understanding. He can't know how much his simple reassurance means to me, how it makes me realize the support I need and would probably have received from Dad if he were alive.

That was the last summer the family lived together. In November Kevin left a winter's worth of wood in the woodshed and a weather-tight roof, and followed his college buddies to San Francisco to work as a carpenter. Jen finished high school over the next two years, tangled in the web of Mom's despair and need, alternately staying close to home to hold Mom together and escaping to be with friends whose families understood how much it was she who needed to be held together.

I went back to college. Attending classes, procrastinating, cramming for finals, manning the front desk at the student union, staying up late—I was exempted from experiencing Mom's neediness on a daily basis. But escape and exemption don't foster recognition or revolution. I maintained the image of my family as perfect—lively, loving, and adventurous—marred only by the tragedy of my father's death at the age of forty-seven. And I didn't question my relationship with my mother.

It was in graduate school for clinical psychology that, in classes, supervision, and therapy, I began to examine my sense of self, my emotional resonance, my role in the family, and my relationship with my mother. The well-practiced inclination to put my mother's feelings before my own became constricting, like one layer of winter clothing too many, to be shed in the mid-day sun. The stranglehold of pity I felt for her loosened.

When I tell my mother that I've decided to see a therapist in order to be a better therapist myself, she says:"That's a good idea.You need a place to talk about Dad." I want her approval, but her response makes me furious. It's bad enough that my psychology professors are suggesting I need therapy for personal reasons. But she has always pushed me away when I wanted to talk about Dad. Now she says I need therapy for it. I feel betrayed—robbed.

My intake appointment is with an imposing psychiatrist in his forties. "Tell me why you are here," he begins. I explain that I'm going to be a clinical psychologist, and that to be a good one, I need to experience therapy myself. He argues that not every therapist needs therapy, especially not at reduced rates when there are plenty of people in the world who really need it. He suggests I not waste his time unless I really have something to deal with. Then he says:"I sense an undercurrent of sadness.What is that about?"

"How does he know?" I wonder. "What can he see?" I hold back my tears and keep my voice calm as I explain about my father's death and how annoyed I am with my mother for suggesting that I need therapy to deal with it. "At the risk of agreeing with your mother," he says at the end of our time, "I think you need therapy to deal with the many feelings you seem to be unaware of—but for yourself, not your professional aspirations." I barely make it out of his office before the tears begin. I give over to wailing sobs in the semiprivacy of my car, grip the steering wheel, and pull out of the parking lot, blinking my eyelashes like windshield wipers.

As soon as I start therapy, Mom rushes in to fix our relationship before I can uncover something.When I tell her that I'm realizing the burden of being the perfect child in the family, she quickly writes to apologize for putting me in that role, to explain that she didn't know it was destructive, and to tell me that I don't have to be perfect anymore.

"You can't take that back now!" I explode over the phone. "It's who I am. I can't become something I'm not, poof, like magic, just to absolve you of your guilt!"

I struggled to free myself from the entanglements in my relationship with my mother; to acknowledge the sadness, anger, and longing that lay beneath my confident facade; and to express them. My attempts to change provoked change-reactions that we could rarely work out between us; both of us were too stubborn, angry, and afraid of rejection to bring it directly to each other.

December 1981
Dear Walter [my mother wrote to an old friend],
    I would like to tell you more about Sara.
    . . . My perception of her is undergoing fairly drastic revision these days. I tend to see her as strong and independent and self-confident and self-sufficient, and not needful of anything I might have to offer (which is exactly the way I viewed Phil right up until shortly before his death).
    . . . So [her] messages have to be crystal clear (as in, "I wish you could make me some cocoa," via long-distance telephone) before I catch on. Just recently she revealed another little corner of her vulnerability, which I haven't yet been able to distill into terms succinct enough to fit into a reasonably sized letter. But when I get it figured out, you'll be the second to know (that puts you behind Connie, but, no doubt, ahead of Sara).
    Jane

Interlude I

Space for Transformation

September 1997

I didn't expect to encounter my inner demons at the ice rink. I often feel as if I don't deserve the ice—that other skaters are entitled to the space they need, while my needs can be deferred, minimized, or eliminated.

At the city rink where I began group lessons, I felt welcomed into a special community. The staff and volunteers were passionate about promoting figure skating and ice hockey among the local kids in a largely African-American neighborhood—and equally committed to skaters of all ages and races. Four orange cones placed at the boundaries of the inner circle of the ice during public sessions created an oasis for practicing spins and crossovers, while rink attendants directed traffic away from the center. Outside this zone of safety, skaters frenetically circled the rink—boys raced by in hockey skates, adolescent girls lurched and laughed and grabbed handfuls of each other's coats before going down in a heap, and adults who'd never skated before squealed with fright as they ventured onto the ice. Young children zigzagged toward the center space, drawn as if by a magnet to our fancy moves. "Wow! How'd you do that? Teach me!" they entreated, before the attendants redirected them outside the cones. I gave quick lessons in gliding or two-footed spinning, ringed by an eager group of children.

Then the city rink closed for the season in late February, and I switched to the University of Pennsylvania's ice rink, skating during the noontime freestyle sessions with serious figure skaters. Unlike public sessions, where dozens of people circumnavigate the rink in a constant flow, only a handful of people skate during freestyle sessions. They crisscross the ice in serpentine patterns and bear down on the four corners for axels, double jumps, and flying camel spins.

During these sessions, I step carefully onto the ice and stroke slowly around the edge, trying to keep out of the way while I warm up. I only relax my vigilance during my lessons, when I can skate with confidence in the atmosphere of safety that my coach creates. He positions himself to protect my lesson space. He demands my effort and focus, points out my progress, inspires me to try harder. During this half hour, my life assumes the shape of adventure.

But when my coach leaves for his next student, the circle of safety dissipates. I feel alone on the ice—awkward, off-balance, lurching, a slave to gravity. I muster the resolve to circle a small corner of the rink and gather courage for a waltz jump, only to abort the move and stagger toward the wall to make way for Stephen, a powerful skater whose toe pick leaves huge divots when he jumps. When it looks safe again, I move out on the ice for another round of three turns—then spot Jackie out of the corner of my eye. She commands the ice with strong, even strokes, and sails high in the air during waltz jumps, her legs extended like the aerial split of a circus performer. She is coming my way, building speed, and I race for the edge again. By the time I venture back to my circle for a set of forward crossovers, Stephen and Jackie have traversed the rink and are headed toward me again—one to land an axel, the other a double salchow. I hug the rails, convinced that I am an annoyance for moving so slowly.

I scan the ice for a better spot. At the other end of the rink, Monica is practicing sit spins. Spinning requires less space than jumping, so this might be a safer place for me. But as I skate toward Monica's end of the rink, Sue catches up with me and attaches herself to my side. A different kind of obstacle on the ice, Sue offers unsolicited advice, shows me her new gloves, asks me to watch her jump, and complains about her job. When I manage to pull out of her orbit, she is snubbed. "You're too serious," she charges, "skating should be social!"

The Zamboni revs. The clock indicates five more minutes in the session, and I'm disheartened. Moves I was beginning to get last week, I've lost. I'll never skate like Stephen or Jackie or even Monica.

At my next lesson, my coach will instruct me on edges and balance, on check and bend and push. But he won't address my feeling of obligation to make way for better skaters, my trouble establishing focus, my difficulty with skaters who talk too much, my tendency to measure myself against others. When he's there I don't have those troubles.

Sitting on the bench to untie my laces and dry my skate blades at the end of practice, I moan to Monica: "I just couldn't get it together today. So many people on the ice. I'm getting worse, not better!"

In her response, and the comments of other skaters who chime in to the conversation, I begin to understand that my problems are universal. All skaters struggle to silence the inner critic, to accept setbacks, to avoid unhelpful comparisons, and to chart their own course. And though no one hands me a rule book, I begin to understand skaters' etiquette—who gets the right of way, how to predict where a skater will jump, how to watch where I'm going, and how to skate so others can antici-pate my movements.

But those rules of accommodation go only so far in helping me claim space on the ice. I need inner focus and determination; I need to give myself permission to take up space; I need to rec-ognize that I have as much right to be there as anyone else. I am so adept at tuning in to the needs of others and so quick to lose my resolve when I think my actions will upset someone that I have trouble honoring my own needs.

As a young girl, I apologized for every wrong note on the piano or flute during my practice sessions, as if my errors were an intrusion on the aural space of others. "Oops, sorry!" rang out from the practice room, whether someone was listening or not. "Why are you apologizing?" my mother asked from time to time. I shrugged. I didn't know. I sometimes dropped the apologies when I realized that no one was within earshot or when, on occasion, I became so engrossed in the music that I lost my customary self-consciousness. But "I'm sorry" was quick to return.

When my own children improvise at the piano, crank up the volume on the electric guitar or bass, or bang away at the drums, I am impressed by their musical confidence. Phillip is fearless in taking control of his instruments. Unperturbed by the notion that others may be disturbed by the noise, his volume is driven by a sense of how the music should sound or by the inner energy and emotion that seeks expression. The piano, the guitar, and the drums are no longer objects when Phillip plays—they are an extension of his self.

In the same way, some skaters don't skate on the ice; they own it. They take it and use it, and in so doing, they transform it.

My tendency to shrink is at play even as I write this book. I credit my former therapist, Margaret, with spurring me to begin writing. She'd helped me work through grief for my father and issues with my mother during my early adulthood, and I hadn't seen her for several years when she happened to call Kenwyn with a question about a referral. It was a few months after my mother's death, and when Kenwyn mentioned that to Margaret, she said: "Why don't you tell Sara to give me a call. I'd like to hear how she's doing."

I made an appointment, drove to her new office in the suburbs, lay on the couch as I had so many times in the past, and began my story.

"That was quite an experience, Sara, and you describe it so well. You should write about it," Margaret interjected as the end of the hour approached.

"You're not the first person to suggest that," I said. "People often say that they get goose bumps when they hear my story. It's happened so often, I call it the goose-bump factor, and it's got me thinking about writing. But whenever I'm in a bookstore and scan the books on grief and loss, death and dying, relationships and spirituality, I find so many books out there already. Who needs one more?"

"Sara," Margaret said emphatically, "there's room on the shelf for your book."

Soon after Margaret announced: "Our time is up. By the way, my fee has gone up since you were last here. It's now a hundred dollars."

I stalled for a moment, pretending to rummage in my bag for my checkbook. I was stunned—not because Margaret had raised her rates but because she was asking me to pay at all. I'd come at her request, I thought. I figured I was giving her the satisfaction of hearing the next chapter in my life, of knowing that she'd helped me grow.

For a moment I considered challenging the payment, but instead I wrote the check and handed it over. "After all, she spent fifty minutes of her professional time with me," I rationalized.

On the drive back to Philadelphia, my decision to pay niggled at me. Why hadn't I been more assertive? Why hadn't I pointed out that we had different expectations for the session? I might have been able to negotiate the fee.

But it was too late.

"I can't get my money back. But maybe there's another way to reconcile this," my thoughts continued. "What about that session is worth a hundred dollars to me?"

Right away I knew.

"There's room on the shelf for your book."

That was the hundred-dollar statement; that was Margaret's gift.

When I got home and sorted through the mail, another gift awaited me. It was a brochure from the University of Pennsylvania announcing spring classes for the general community. "Writing from Personal Experience" was a six-week seminar that caught my eye, and I immediately picked up the phone to register.

Two weeks later I was writing.

My skating coach, my old therapist, my fellow skaters, and students in my writing class all urge me to establish myself, to act from my center, to carve the space I need to develop my talents. Who am I to keep those gifts in their original boxes with the tissue paper still wrapped around them, hoarding them out of insecurity or fear or false modesty?

My challenge on the ice or at the writing desk, as it was with caring for my mother, is both an outer and an inner battle. Along with putting my claim on space and time in a physical sense, I must work to create inner space—to clear my mind of the clutter of judgmental attitudes, self-criticism, fear, and doubt—to make room for God at the center. In a sense it is reclamation, for we are all made in the image of the divine and filled with sacred light and love. And yet we seem to forget, to crowd out or shade that light.

The delight of recognizing the indwelling spirit, whether in the middle of a centered spin, engrossed in the creative process of writing, or in silence, demands a bolder response than just appreciative applause from the sidelines. It calls us to greater stillness, deeper commitment, and broader communion. It moves us to see the divine in all, judging ourselves neither less nor more precious in God's eyes than anyone else.

Chapter 6

The Recovery Agenda

February 1996

Mom complains that she can't remember what the oncologist told her. She wants me to clarify, then scowls at my explanations. She says, "Maybe we should call Dawn," her pathologist friend from the day-care center, who had offered to be her medical advocate.

Dawn visits Mom after working hours. She begins by asking her what she knows and how she understands the information she's been given. Mom's answers are brief and slightly off track. Has she forgotten what the oncologist said, or is she hoping she misunderstood? When Dawn explains the diagnosis gently, in simple terms, Mom feels more hopeful, though it doesn't seem to me that the message has changed.

As I walk down the hall with Dawn, I comment on how generous she is with her time. With two young children and a demanding career, she must be as busy as I am. Sensing my curiosity she explains: "I have always enjoyed your mother. But I have to admit that there is something more. When I was a first-year medical student, my mother was diagnosed with terminal breast cancer. She became angry and bitter as treatment after treatment failed. She pushed my brother and me away; she didn't want us meddling. She and my father fought. The rifts in my family didn't heal before she died. When I see you and your brother and sister caring for your mother, I see so much love. You are pulling together, not falling apart."

Maybe Dawn is right—despite the divisive forces in our family, we are coming together. Our complicated history doesn't matter when Mom asks for the bedpan or for more ice or reaches for my hand. Having decided to be Mom-focused, her self-absorption doesn't annoy me, and I'm not plagued by old longings for her attention and understanding.

The morning after Dawn's visit, Mom asks: "Sara, am I doing this right? I feel like I'm supposed to fight and I'm supposed to grieve and I'm supposed to make amends and I'm supposed to enjoy what time I have left and I'm supposed to make decisions! How can I do all that?"

"Oh, Mom," I choke back tears. "You are doing it right. All those things are important, but you don't have to do them all today."

It seems she doesn't really want to do any of this fighting or grieving or reconciling or deciding. In recent days she has been withdrawing. She brightens briefly when a visitor or a new flower arrangement arrives, then retreats to the safety of the morphine button, the TV remote control, or sleep. She greets the social worker, the cancer support counselor, the nurse specialists, but won't talk about the real issues, ask questions, or make commitments. A pile of unread pamphlets is growing on her bedside table: "Coping with Cancer," "Finding the Support You Need," "Patient Rights and Responsibilities."

I watch the tug-of-war between my mother and the hospital staff—the more she withdraws or resists, the more they push. I understand the hospital staff's agenda. I understand Mom's exhaustion and fear. I sit in the middle and coax.

One battleground is the electronic breathing gadget, which arrived within eighteen hours of surgery. "Come on, Mom, let's try this again." I proffer the breathing tube. She is supposed to attempt ten deep breaths every twenty minutes to keep her lungs clear and reduce the risk of secondary infection. "Not right now," she growls at me. "Take that thing away." She has barely mustered one weak blow in the last three hours. I wait a few minutes, and offer the tube again. Though I have little success, I keep urging, even during her friend's visit, hoping she'll do it to look good or not raise a fuss. But I've miscalculated. "How did I manage to raise a Nazi for a daughter?" she appeals to her friend with biting sarcasm. "Don't let that sweet-looking exterior fool you!"

Her protests when asked to walk are even more vigorous. "How do they expect me to walk? I can't walk under the best of circumstances. My legs will buckle. My surgical staples will pull," she moans. "I wish Kevin were here. He'd just pick me up and move me from the bed to the chair."

Though I pressure Mom to comply with staff requests, I am also her advocate in this complex, multidisciplinary system that often sabotages its own efforts to care and heal. I intervene when she is kept waiting for medication or the bedpan because the unit is short-staffed. I post a "do not disturb" sign on her door, and stave off the residents, medical students, social workers, phlebotomists, breathing specialists, student nurses, and telephone bill collectors who arrive to interrupt her nap. I nurture my relationships with staff, learning their different roles and personalities, establishing their trust in me, and negotiating access to resources like clean linens, a VCR, or extra pillows.

Mom is deeply appreciative of my support even as she complains. Perhaps knowing she can lean on me gives her the freedom to be cranky. And maybe being cranky keeps her from being despondent.

Although I am caught up in the here and now, focused on the immediacy of Mom's physical needs, and although I am convinced that she has many months to live, the certainty of her death creates a constant, dragging undercurrent that I feel unprepared to face. I begin collecting books about death and dying, and hide them in my suitcase so Mom won't see the titles. I read with gruesome fascination Sherwin Nuland's book *How We Die,* learning about the physical experience of dying from heart attack, stroke, cancer, and other causes. But I set the book aside before I've finished, disillusioned by its lack of attention to the emotional and spiritual experience of dying. Dawn lends me *Death and Dignity,* by Timothy Quill, and I grow angry about how death has been institutionalized, the rights of patients stripped, the experience dehumanized. I wish that the caring man that wrote that book and works in this hospital could be my mother's doctor.

A friend sends me Henri Nouwen's book *Our Greatest Gift: A Meditation on Dying and Caring.* I spread my fingers to hide the title, and read, "To care for the dying is to keep saying, 'You are the beloved daughter of God.'" My mother's emotional and spiritual needs are as vital as her physical needs. I glance at her as she naps, and wonder if she could hear "God loves you."

My mother and I rarely discuss God or religion. She comes to church with my family when she visits—I'm not sure if it's out of politeness, nostalgia, or current interest. As a child she went to synagogue a few times with her father's relatives and to a Protestant church once a year on Easter Sunday with her mother. Neither set of experiences created a grounded faith or even a sense of familiarity. When she married she joined my father in attending the Methodist church, drawn along by his faith, conviction, and involvement. We were a family who attended church every Sunday for most of my childhood. But after Dad died, Mom grew cynical, bitter, and angry with a God who could allow his death and worse in the world. I don't know if now she considers herself agnostic, atheistic, or simply disinterested.

I don't think Mom can hear "God loves you."

And I'm not sure I can say it.

In Sunday school and at church camp, I listened to Bible stories, sang "Jesus Loves Me," and glued brightly colored construction paper letters onto white newsprint to spell "God Is Love." In what J. Phillip Newell refers to as the Big Book of Creation, I walked down the middle of streams that flowed through the woods on the farm, cool water swirling around my ankles and squishing through the holes of my old sneakers. Overhead the trees announced their brave seasonality—summer's abundant green giving way to fall's fiery extravaganza, and winter's stark branches yielding to the pale green breath of spring. I sensed God in the swirling waters, the fiery leaves, the stark gray branches, and the pale green breath.

But when my father's heart gave out, the anchor of my young faith was gone. My mother, who had learned to walk twice in her life already, was reduced to a crawl. And who was I? Perennial ray of sunshine? My mother's crutch? The family pacemaker? Or brokenhearted and crawling myself?

In college I set religion on the intellectual chopping block; studied philosophy, anthropology, history, and psychology; and dismissed faith as an expression of the universal propensity to believe in something bigger than oneself. I put my trust in the mind, the will.

My relationship with Kenwyn drew me to the church again. We found our way to First Presbyterian Church in Philadelphia, attracted to the richly textured preaching, broad thinking, and Scottish brogue of Dr. Ernest Somerville. His sermons were like a set of stepping stones laid in a rushing stream—every listener, whether devout or in doubt, could find a stone within reach of a searching foot. We were married by Dr. Somerville at First Presbyterian, and mourned his sudden death from a heart attack nine months later. We celebrated the births and baptisms of our children in that congregation. Then, feeling spiritually undernourished by the pastor who replaced Dr. Somerville, we sought a new church, and found Bryn Mawr Presbyterian, where I continued to search for stepping stones along the path to deeper faith.

With my uncertainties about faith and my mother's sense of abandonment and anger, how can I speak to her of God's love?

Yet as I read on in Nouwen's small, profound book, I realize that I am already telling her—"through words, prayers, and blessings;

through gentle touch and the holding of hands; through cleaning and feeding; through listening and just being there."

He calls it "practicing the ministry of presence."

Practicing the ministry of presence, letting God's love flow between us, involves sacrifice. To be physically present in this moment, I've left my children, husband, and job behind in Philadelphia. To be emotionally receptive, I've set aside my anxiety, grief, fatigue, and old anger so my feelings don't crowd hers.

It is not that I am free of those emotions. As I observe the generosity, love, and caring that characterizes Mom's relationships with others, I am jealous and filled with longing. Mom's friends share their problems with her, and she gives them comfort and advice. They happily listen to her stories and struggles, cheerfully carry her groceries into the house and empty her garbage as they come and go. Her relationship with my sister-in-law is easygoing and loving. When I comment on this, she explains, "I decided when Kevin got married that I would try to be as good a mother-in-law to Tina as mine was to me." Grandma Corse made Mom feel more loved and accepted than her own mother did, and I can tell that Mom has succeeded in her commitment to love Tina the same way.

But my relationship with Mom is clogged with so much emotional detritus that simple loving has been nearly impossible. Mom often seems to be jealous of me, intimidated by my accomplishments, and afraid of my anger. And I have felt intimidated by her, afraid of the sting of her anger.

As I watch how charming she is with Tina and with all her other friends, how loving and giving, I wonder why it can't be that way between us, and why she didn't make the commitment to love and accept my husband.

It had started out fine.

April 1983

Dear Sara,

It was such a lovely weekend that I want to get my thanks—and my thoughts—down on paper. It was marred only by your feeling so yucky. But aside from that, it was such a pleasure to see you looking—and being—so happy. Ken is such a really nice person—I enjoyed his company and getting to know him a little bit. I know that this is very early on in what Ken refers to as your "fledgling relationship." But should that relationship grow and deepen and endure, it would surely do so with my blessing.

All day long I have had something nagging at the edge of my consciousness, and I finally got hold of it. When I was writing to tell [my friend] Natalie that I was married, I described Phil thusly. "After a long series of boys, I have finally found a man." In that respect I guess Ken reminds me of Dad. And Phil was barely twenty-five at that time, so you see, it doesn't necessarily have anything to do with how old you are. Enjoy!

Love, Mom

Kenwyn and I spent Christmas with Mom that first year. Our visit was mostly nice, but we tussled. I was annoyed with Mom for continually complaining about my brother and sister, who'd both changed their plans and not come for Christmas. In focusing on who hadn't come, if felt as if she was unable to appreciate who had. "Hey," I said at one point, "We're the ones who came! Stop complaining to us!" And I watched Kenwyn struggle with feeling excluded during the many conversations that featured inside jokes and idiosyncratic family humor. When Mom tried to entertain Kenwyn with stories about my early boyfriends, as if he were a kindly uncle, I was furious. She was miffed when I asked her to stop.

Back at the university after the break, I noticed a change in my weekly phone conversations with Mom. "Don't you find Kenwyn intimidating . . . controlling . . . terribly serious . . . ?" "Isn't there quite a big age difference between you?" she asked, seemingly unaware of the divisiveness of her negative commentary about him. I fumed, and finally got up the nerve to confront her.

"You may have whatever reactions you want to Kenwyn," I asserted, trying to control my shaky voice, "but you cannot express them to me."

I was surprised by the forcefulness of my *no,* and pleased that her comments about Kenwyn stopped.

Since beginning therapy in the second semester of my first year of graduate school, I had been questioning my relationship with my mother. As I came to the realization that I had silenced my own needs and emotions to keep the peace and be the good little girl who took care of Mom's emotional needs, I began to recognize the longing to be heard and understood that I had long suppressed. At the same time that I tapped into this childhood longing for closeness with my mother, I became aware of why I kept my distance—both in the present and as a young girl. Along with placing a boundary around my relationship with Kenwyn to keep my mother's opinions, issues, and projections from suffusing my feelings for him, I built walls around my own development. I was suspicious of her interest in my psychological process, and equally suspicious of her wish to tell me about hers.

March 31, 1984

Dear Mom,

My not wanting to be close is not wanting to wallow around in each other's self-analytic life. We have therapists and friends for that. I may, as you suggested, want to know about your history and your thoughts about our family "for its historical value" someday. But not now. Why don't you write it in a book, and I can read it when I'm forty or something.

. . . Everybody needs to tell their own story. And everyone likes to have someone to tell it to, but I can't be your audience right now.

I get the feeling you want to tell me these things to fix it— so I'll understand and not be mad and tell you I forgive you. But I don't blame you—I don't feel like you've committed some grave wrong that needs my forgiveness. That doesn't mean I'm not angry. But there's a difference between my being angry and my blaming you . . . In order for me to work this through, I need to come to my own private understanding and acceptance of what life's about for me, including your place in it.

As my relationship with Kenwyn deepened and became more committed, I opened up a bit more with my mother. I wanted us to have some of the closeness that is associated with wedding planning and celebrating the transition to married life. In a letter designed, I think, to bless our union, Mom was particularly straightforward about her underlying issues.

January 1985
Dear Sara,
     . . . I am happy for you and Ken in your decision to get married . . .
     In the natural progression of things, each generation of a family surpasses the one before it. My mother graduated from high school, which was quite an accomplishment for a person of her economic status at that time. Dad and I were the first ones in our families to go to college. And you will be the first to earn a doctorate!
     My mother was the one in her family who "left home" to go to work—fifty miles away in Chicago! Phil and I at various times made our homes many more than fifty miles from our origins. And now you are embarking on a life that is literally international.
     My pride in you and your accomplishments is virtually boundless. My love for you is total and unconditional.
     We have discussed at least once before that my happiness for you is marred by twinges of envy. I consider this a most unadmirable trait in myself, but I realize that beneath it lies the fear that as you move ahead in your life, I will somehow get left behind.
     Love, Mom

I appreciated her affirmation and support, and her acknowledgment of her envy and fear of abandonment. It felt easy to receive such a straightforward gift.

But more often my mother had trouble being direct with her feelings. Instead of addressing conflict, her anger slipped out in the form of barbs that were easy to miss, though you noticed the sting. Or it was transformed into a "poor me," and I would be drawn to feel sorry for her or guilty for not making her feel better. On the eve of my wedding, my mother couldn't give me the simple gifts of her affirmation and support, or the more challenging gift of containing her own issues.

June 1985

"Why don't you check on how the bathroom repair is coming?" I shout to Kenwyn over the sound of the vacuum cleaner as he lumbers past carrying an armchair.

Our wedding is tomorrow, with the reception for ninety guests in our new home. Aside from shopping for a wedding dress in February, sending out invitations, and scheduling the church for the ceremony, Kenwyn and I left wedding planning to the last minute. Proving the bridal magazines wrong, we found a caterer, photographer, string quartet, DJ, vocalist, florist, and furniture rentals in three weeks, and embarked on major house and garden improvements as well, all while working full-time. As Kenwyn rearranges furniture for dancing and dining, the caterer drops by to assess the space in our oven, a friend plants annuals to add color to our garden, the workmen spackle the bathroom, and I frantically clean. My family will arrive at any moment from out of town.

Kenwyn glances out the big picture window in the dining room and sees the cars pulling up to the curb. "They're here!"

Mom, Jenny, Kevin, Tina, and Connie burst into the house with noise and energy. I greet them happily, though I feel too harried to play hostess. I find a chair for Mom by the dining-room window, invite people to help themselves to drinks from the refrigerator, and go off in search of my dust cloth. With a sweeping glance of the room to assess my progress and decide what absolutely has to be done next, I notice everyone is clustered around Mom, rubbing her shoulder and passing her tissues. She is sobbing. "What's wrong?" I ask, expecting disaster. But no one is listening to me. Snippets of conversation come through: "I wish your father were here . . . first wedding . . . he should be making this speech . . . why me?"

I back away, hardening myself against the tears, determined not to add "make Mom feel better" to my extensive to-do list.

Why did she wait until she landed in my dining room to fall apart? Can't she see what's going on in this house? This is my event.

If anyone should be crying about Dad, it's me. But he's been dead for over eight years. He's missed my college graduation, getting to know my friends, celebrating my acceptance to graduate school, hearing about my blunders and achievements. This is only the next thing.

I turn my back on Mom, my shoulders set.

"What needs cleaning next?" Connie asks, reaching for the vacuum cleaner, and I feel a rush of gratitude.

In my dream Mom arrives at my house the day before I am to be married. She takes my face between her two soft hands, smiles tenderly, looks me in the eye, and says: "I love you, sweetie. I wish your father were here to see you marry, to walk you down the aisle. He would be so proud of you." She asks me how I am. She wants to know if there's anything she can do to help. She says, "Where's Kenwyn; where's my wonderful son-in-law to be?"

But I'm not dreaming. Mom is locked in her own grief and anger, and pulls whoever she can into her swirling whirlpool of emotion. I steel myself.

Despite her breakdown, Mom pulled it together and enjoyed the rehearsal dinner she had generously offered to host. She made a brief and tearful but sweet speech, welcoming Kenwyn into the family, acknowledging his parents, who weren't able to travel from Australia for the wedding, and saying how proud she was of me. People had a good time.

That night Grandma Corse, Mom, Jenny, Connie, and my friend Ana—my bridal party—stayed with me at a nearby hotel.

While getting ready the next morning, however, another magnetic force field formed around my mother as she tugged at each of us in turn to affirm that her dress looked fine, her crooked hips and mismatched legs didn't show too much, her shoes didn't look stupid, her eyeliner was straight, her nail color was right. I was grateful when Ana and Connie took me by the elbow and extricated me from Mom's room. In the relative peace of my room, they fussed with my hair and makeup, zipped my dress, adjusted my veil, and told me I was a beautiful bride. My grandmother watched and smiled.

At the church my shy, countrified Uncle Dave, nine years my father's junior, proudly but nervously walked me down the aisle. My sister was a beautiful, attentive bridesmaid. The music was soul-filled, as were my husband's eyes as we said, "I do." After the ceremony our friends spilled out onto Walnut Street on a beautiful June day, while the photographer kept the bridal party behind to take pictures in the sanctuary. When Kenwyn and I appeared at the top of the steps to the church, the gathering burst into spontaneous applause and cheers. Back at the house, we danced and danced in the nicely vacuumed dining room.

My mother seemed to hold herself together through the wedding and reception, though I kept a safe enough distance that I wouldn't find out if my impression was wrong. I tried my best to forget her emotional hemorrhage, along with my wishful dream of the doting mother.

That night Kenwyn and I stayed in Shirl's Shed, a tiny cottage bordering a wood in a suburb north of Philadelphia. In the morning deer watched us from behind the trees as we ate croissants and jam on the patio. When we returned home that night, the family was gone.

But a few days later, Kenwyn received a letter from my mother in the mail. "Oh, dear," he said as he finished reading and handed it to me. Mom wrote that she found Kenwyn intimidating, that he was unresponsive when she welcomed him into the family, and that she hoped she would learn to read his reactions as loving, just as she came to accept that Kevin shows his caring in ways other than what she hopes for or expects.

The letter felt jarring and confusing—a letter bomb. We decided to call her and tell her how it upset us.

"You've misunderstood," she said defensively. "I'm not blaming you. I'm saying I want us to have a better relationship."

But I was still angry about the emotional hurricane she brought to my wedding. I couldn't see her good intentions, only the hostility.

At the same time, I was torn between loyalty to my husband—who recognized the barbs embedded in my mother's surface communications, demanded more direct and authentic communication, and wanted to shelter me from hurts I couldn't always acknowledge—and my lingering investment in my family's way of being. I felt guilty when my mother complained of being misunderstood or victimized by our demands for her to change.

Six weeks later Kenwyn and I left the swirl of tensions associated with separating from my family of origin and headed for Australia—to enter the swirl of *his* family. We celebrated our wedding with a mini-reenactment ceremony at the home of his friends, worked together as consultants at an Australian organization, and enjoyed a few days of honeymooning in Fiji on our way home.

Chapter 7

Amniotic

February 1996

Mom is adrift in her hospital bed, caught in powerful currents of depression and lethargy. She doesn't seem to mind drifting. The hospital staff has indoctrinated me in the paradigm of active recovery, but Mom is not such an easy convert. She vacillates between resisting all requests for her cooperation and counting on my optimism and energy to drag her along. It makes me nervous. When will she take responsibility for her own healing? Just when I consider pushing harder or maybe backing off completely to give her the impetus to move forward herself, she says: "I know what I need to do, Sara. I'm just not ready yet."

A promise of change. It hooks me, and I continue to care for her in the way she finds acceptable.

Throughout my early adulthood, I clamored for my mother to change. We exchanged agonized letters, we interspersed bravely mustered confrontations with periods of wound-licking avoidance. We alternated between keeping things superficial and pushing for greater connection. At times it seems we moved in the general direction of a better relationship, but our efforts were labored and progress was minimal.

Becoming a mother myself increased my commitment to getting along with my mother—but also my zeal for new terms. I didn't want the difficulties in our relationship to affect how my children experienced their grandmother, and I had less tolerance for my mother's unacknowledged emotional manipulations.

It was a pregnancy complicated by constant morning sickness—and then the thrilling but startling news that I was carrying twins. Mom called me frequently, sometimes worried about my health but often just eager to share her ideas. For years she had worked to contain her eagerness for grandchildren so as not to be seen as pressuring her children. But with the role of wife wrested away from her too soon, her adult children keeping their distance, and her relationships with the children at the day-care center necessarily circumscribed, she had been longing to find new meaning in life as a grandmother. Now she was free to let her excitement brim over. She looked with new interest at all the latest baby equipment, books by parenting experts, toys, and articles on pregnancy and birth. She talked a lot about how things had changed since she was a young mother. She expressed regret that she hadn't felt truly present at the births of her three children. She hinted that she wanted to witness the births of her twin grandbabies.

But I couldn't let her come that close. She would have to be content with the story.

August 1987

I feel a funny pop and sudden wetness, leap from the bed, and race to the bathroom with an agility I haven't experienced since early in my pregnancy. "I think this is it. I think my water just broke." What a funny phrase!

Kenwyn is awake in an instant.

Seven hours later my first baby slithers into the world, and I reach for this slippery gift with the wiggling arms and legs.

"Oh, my God, it's a baby," I blurt out, laughing.

Was I expecting a bunny?

Justin's slick skin is warm and wet; it yields to my protective touch. Before I can hold him in my arms, he is whisked off to be measured, footprinted, examined. The activity around him intensifies, but I hear only one word—lungs—and the clattering wheels of the bassinet as they roll him to the neonatal intensive care unit for observation.

A drama is still in progress in my womb.

"Baby B heartbeat dropping," barks the obstetric resident, her stethoscope pressing on my belly. The midwife steps to one side as the obstetrician who serves as his emergency backup leaps toward me with her hands outstretched; it is a finely choreographed dance. "This is going to hurt," she warns as she reaches in to ensure that the umbilical cord is not wrapped around the baby's neck.

"Vacuum," she orders, stretching her free hand behind her. "Sara, with your next contraction, this baby is going to be born."

This time the energy around the bassinet does not escalate, there are no low admonitions regarding breath sounds, no trip to the intensive care. Baby B passes his Apgar test, is cleaned and swaddled and placed in my arms. I am encouraged to nurse him, and Kenwyn goes to check on Justin. He returns with reassurances and awe.

Twenty-four hours later, two bundles nestle in my arms.

"One of them is named Justin, but we haven't settled on the second name," we tell friends and family. Will we call him Phillip, after my father? Or would that burden him with history, upset my mother, or set him apart from his brother?

When I talk with my Grandma Corse, I don't mention that I'm considering the name she gave her firstborn son. She and I have spent the summer worrying about each other—I on bed rest in Philadelphia, she recovering from a stroke in Sandy Creek. I don't want to disappoint her if we decide on a different name. "I'm so proud of you, sweetie. Two babies, and the right sex, too," she teases. As a mother of three sons, she's always been openly partial to boys—reframing her lot in life as a matter of personal choice.

Mom calls to say she's coming to Philadelphia; she can't wait to hold her first grandchildren.

On the day we will go home from the hospital, I awake from my best night of sleep; the adrenaline of birthing is finally wearing off. I feed the boys and swaddle them in clean cotton blankets. I tell the nurse to fill out Phillip's birth certificate; we have decided on the name. I am giddy with excitement.

When Kenwyn arrives to take us home, he asks me to sit—there is sympathy in his eyes. His tone is sober.

"I just got a call from your mother. It is your Grandma Corse. She had another stroke and died this morning."

Through my tears I moan to Kenwyn, "But I never got to tell her about the name, about Phillip!"

She's gone, and it's too late to send a message to my father, I think, as if I could have wrapped this news in a handkerchief and pressed it in her palm as she passed by.

The next day my mother arrives, and Kenwyn settles her in the middle of the couch with a baby in each arm. She gazes at one, then the other, filled to bursting with newborn love at the same time that she is grieving the death of her beloved mother-in-law.

With the babies less than a week old, we drive to Sandy Creek for my grandmother's funeral. Sadness and joy intermingle.

My mother was delighted in her new role as grandmother, and I was delighted in her delight. Becoming a mother made me appreciate what it must have been like for her to raise three children after polio. At the same time, I was determined not to make the mistakes she made in mothering me, and I was critical of her. Though I found it difficult to speak up against my mother when she said or did something that hurt me or that I thought was destructive for her, I became ferocious in motherhood, developing the protective instinct that makes it dangerous to come between a mother bear and her cubs.

"Look at your old fumble-fingered grandma," Mom says to one-month-old Justin, trying to push his tiny fist through the sleeve of his pajamas. She uses a high-pitched voice that babies love; a smile flutters across his face.

"How did she ever manage to raise three children when she can't even put this shirt on you?"

I know Mom is joking; it is even kind of funny. But there's too much behind the joke. She wants my attention, my laughter. She wants me to refute her, to say:"Oh, no, Mom, you're not a fumble-fingered grandmother. You're great! You did a great job of raising your three children." But I'm not giving it to her when she drops hints. I was up three times last night to feed the babies—I don't need another hungry soul sucking at me.

I chew her comment over in my mind for almost an hour before managing to say:"Please don't put yourself down in front of the babies, Mom. I don't want them to grow up hearing you talk about yourself that way." Stifling a giggle on the one hand and hurt and anger on the other, my mother settles for pursed lips in response.

I have adopted psychologically aware mothering of the late twentieth century, and fail to see any humor in my statement.

As my mother grew into the grandmothering role, she established a comfort zone. She folded endless piles of laundry, helped make dinner, baked cinnamon swirl bread and apple pie. She enjoyed the antics of the children and affirmed the way I mothered. However, she made her limits clear. She was happy to rock a contented infant, but not one in distress. She refused to change diapers, worried she'd stab a baby with a diaper pin. She didn't feel comfortable being alone with the boys, so couldn't offer to babysit. She enjoyed reading aloud—the books that she found appealing—but not playing pretend or building with Legos.

I appreciated what Mom did do, but though I understood her limits, I silently railed against them. Each time she visited, I seemed to renew my expectations that she might rock and burp and change diapers and play and feed and read and take care of me and babysit, so I could rest and Kenwyn and I might go out to dinner or a movie. I tried to broaden the role that she carved out for herself, thinking it was just a matter of her getting used to the idea and developing confidence. I resented that my role as a mother had to include taking care of her—helping her establish a good relationship with the children and feel good about herself as a grandmother.

I started working full-time when the boys were fifteen months old, and the stress and busyness in my life intensified. My mother seemed to envy all that I had—a career as a psychologist, young children, a husband, a nice house, money to travel—while I felt sorry for her—lonely, unfulfilled, bereft, financially struggling, emotionally needy. I alternated between sharing the good things in my life, in search of her acknowledgment and affirmation, and hiding them, so she wouldn't feel jealous, presenting my struggles instead: "I have a grant deadline and have to work late all week" or "The boys kept us up all night" or "Justin has a rash" or "The babysitter is driving me crazy." "Look at the tough things in my life," I would say, holding them out on a platter for all to see. "Please make me feel better."

Our third child came into being with less effort than the first two. No worries about fertility, no months of trying, no ultrasounds. Yet despite the ease of conception, managing severe nausea that lasted from early morning until bedtime while working full-time, studying for the psychology licensure exam, and mothering two two-year-old boys threatened to flatten me. For weeks I gritted my teeth, unable to handle the stress of a minor disagreement between the boys, the smell of onions cooking, or a lively dinner-table conversation. I fled the dining-room table each night, sometimes in the middle of someone's sentence, to hide behind my licensure test preparation manual, quell my queasy stomach, and to push away the panic brought on by a recurrent thought: "How can I have another baby when I have no patience for the two I have? What kind of a mother am I?"

"We need you, Sara," Kenwyn said firmly one day. "You can't disappear on us."

I don't know if it was that wake-up call, the hormonal shift that occurs at fourteen-and-a-half weeks of pregnancy, meeting my grant deadline, passing my licensing exam, or all four, but the second and third trimesters of pregnancy were joyful. My faith in myself as a mother and my delight in Justin and Phillip returned. My conversations with my mother were no longer about what meal I lost in what bathroom during the day, and our relationship was peaceful. She joined us for a week of summer vacation on Lake George; we enjoyed watching the boys develop language and humor, and we laughed at their antics.

"Somersault!" said Justin as he tucked his head and rolled forward across the bed. "Winterpepper!" said Phillip as he lay on his back and flung his feet over his head in an attempt at a backward roll.

With this pregnancy Mom didn't ask to be present at the birth.

I wake from a deep sleep, and am surprised it's only midnight. I doze off, but wake after an hour, again with the sensation that I've slept through the night. Something isn't right. Am I in labor?

Too restless to sleep, I wander downstairs. Struck by the mess in the playroom, I set to reorganizing it with suspicious energy.

Now I feel it. Not just energy, but a tightening in my abdomen.

I'll just finish this job. I'll let Kenwyn sleep.

I last an hour.

"Honey. I'm sorry to wake you."

"What!" Kenwyn is alert in an instant, or seems to be alert.

"I think I'm in labor."

"No you're not," he says. "I have to teach all day tomorrow."

"I know, sweetie. But I think I'm having contractions."

"I blocked out all next week for you to go into labor! The baby's not due for another ten days!"

That is why I think he may not be so alert.

I call the midwife, who suggests I take a shower, time my contractions, and call back when they're five minutes apart.

The shower feels good. I help get the boys up and ready for preschool; I answer the doorbell to one of the carpenters who is renovating our hallway. When he asks how I'm doing, I answer casually. "Fine. I'm in labor."

"What?" he says, and takes a step back.

"It's okay," I say. "It's not contagious."

I make the boys' lunches, leaning against the kitchen counter every few minutes and grimacing. The babysitter drives the boys to school while Kenwyn takes me to the hospital.

The birthing suite is equipped with a Jacuzzi, large, homey bedrooms, a kitchenette, and a living room. No chrome, no stirrups, no need to lie flat on my back strapped to monitors. When the contractions get stronger and the thought of painkillers crosses my mind, the midwife announces that I'm in transition, and I know I can make it.

The head crowns, and the midwife asks, "Would you like to catch the baby?" Kenwyn steps forward. Later he will tell me that in that moment, he envisioned his life stretching out before him along two different paths: the testosterone-loaded path of a family with three boys and one with the balancing energy of a female. He is so prepared for a boy, he thinks at first that that is what he sees.

"It's a girl," he crows as he notices that he was wrong.

Kalila is pink and healthy and beautiful—a perfect ten on the Apgar scale.

Within a few minutes, I am walking around the birthing suite, powered by an adrenaline rush, grinning at others in labor, giddy, foolishly offering to deliver another baby for someone. "You see, I'm used to having two at a time."

When Mom and Jen came to meet Kalila a few days after her birth, and in subsequent visits over the next few years, I began to recognize that though I sometimes felt critical of my mother for how she acted as a grandmother, her grandmothering was not inadequate at all. She loved and laughed and cuddled with the children. She carried pictures of them wherever she went, sharing stories of their development and exploits with friends and colleagues. She scanned reviews and store displays for books they would appreciate at each stage, and polled parents and teachers at the day-care center to find out what toys and activities were popular for children of their age. She devised strategies for fostering her relationships with them from a distance, such as buying double copies of books so she could read aloud to them over the phone while they looked at the pictures. She was a fine grandmother.

What I really wished for was different mothering for myself. And though I shared my present-day trials with her, seeking comfort and understanding, I never was truly satisfied with her responses. It wasn't really today's pain that needed soothing. It was yesterday's.

"Mommy, can you fix my bike?" six-year-old Justin runs in, interrupting my cleaning and my conversation with my mother, who's visiting us for Mother's Day weekend. She's taken up residence at her favorite spot in the house—the old wooden church pew in the kitchen—where she can read and chat and keep tabs on whatever's going on in the family.

I put the chain back on Justin's bike; then, holding my greasy hands away from my white shirt, I walk past the man who is painting our dining room. "I have something to help you clean that," he says, pulling a tub of gunk from his crate of paints, brushes, and turpentine.

Slathering the gunk on my hands, I catch its odor. My heart quickens with pleasure at an old memory. I rush to my mother, grinning. "Hey, Mom! This smells just like Dad!"

As I stretch my hands toward her nose, she wrinkles it in disgust and turns away. "There are other smells I prefer to remember your father by."

Beneath my image of self-sufficiency, equanimity, and empathy, I yearned to be taken care of, to be known, and to feel. My facade as the good daughter was mutually created, bound up in my need for acknowledgment and my mother's need for affirmation as a good mother. As we tried to stretch beyond the confines of that relationship, we both felt endangered. We fought battles and we called truces. We made progress and we regressed.

Then one summer evening, six months before we knew anything about the cancer, Mom and I went out on Long Lake for a
row in the boat, and a profound shift took place inside me.

August 1995

*Mom is planted on the couch, reading. Her crutches lean against the lamp
table, and four or five novels and a book of* New York Times *crossword
puzzles are piled next to her. She comes prepared to entertain herself
whenever she visits, in case she can't keep up with the physical activity.
Her head inclines toward the open window, and a tease of the breeze off
the lake lifts the short, gray curls at the nape of her neck.*

*I think for a moment of yesterday, when Mom settled on the floor with
Justin to play a game he made up, filliping small plastic game pieces
toward the corner pockets of a wooden carom board. "You're hopeless at
this, Grandma," he finally announced with a grin, after a piece she tried
to launch flew backward and landed in her lap. He patiently repeated his
demonstration, and my mother surprised me by asking him for another
rundown of his rapidly evolving rules for judging and scoring each shot.
"How about I give you a handicap," Justin suggested. Mom laughed, and
agreed it was probably a good idea.*

*I have already sacrificed a late-afternoon swim to make dinner, and
can't wait to escape the jumble of dirty dishes to go outside and enjoy an
Adirondack sunset. "Hey, Mom! Come for a row in the boat with me," I
say—an impulsive invitation that evokes an impulsive response.*

*"I'd love to go," Mom blurts out, reaching instinctively toward her
crutches. She hesitates in midstretch. "I'm not sure I can drag myself down
to the dock and back again one more time today."*

"Sure you can," I encourage, glancing at Kenwyn. "We'll help."

*Mom pulls herself to the edge of the couch, slips her arms through the
leather cuffs of the crutches, and heaves herself upright. She leans heavily
on my arm to maneuver the stairs; I feel guilty that we've never installed
a stair railing for her.*

*Our summer cottage sits on a small point of land that juts into Long
Lake. Mom walks the few yards from the house to the wide stone stairway*

that leads to the beach, while I grab life jackets and oars. Clutching both crutches in one hand, Mom grips Kenwyn's arm with the other, and places her feet carefully as she walks down the steps. When she reaches soft sand, she struggles for balance, then relaxes her hold on Kenwyn as she steps onto the wooden dock. Climbing into the boat is another hurdle, but she holds both our hands, lifts her leg over the side, and exhales onto the middle bench, where she settles like ballast. I jump in after her, and Kenwyn launches us onto the lake.

I pull on one oar to turn the boat northward. Several half-grown ducklings paddle toward shore. They thrust their slender heads underwater in search of snails and small fish, leaving a triangle of tail feathers quivering above water to mark their location. When the mother spots us, she quacks a warning to her young.

"Would you like to row for a bit?"

"I wonder if I still can! I used to love to row on Gages Lake."

With none of the awkwardness of her walking, my mother establishes a graceful rhythm with the oars. Her lower body rests deferentially on the bench as she leans into each stroke; her shoulders and back remember the familiar forward bend and pull against the resistance of the water. Rowing is a rare opportunity for Mom to display physical prowess.

Every pull on the oars seems to elicit a memory, and Mom reminisces about her girlhood summers on Gages Lake.

"Aunt Elsie made the four cousins matching sunsuits for us to wear each year. Like the glow-in-the-dark lightning bug T-shirts I gave the grandchildren last year."

I nod and murmur in response, though she isn't really paying attention to me.

"We used to water-ski on a large wooden board pulled behind Uncle Hilmer's pokey little powerboat. I had good balance, and was a bit of a daredevil." Mom's voice is soft and distant as she recalls the days before polio.

"Sometimes my sister and I felt like second-class citizens. After all, Aunt Elsie and Uncle Hilmer were doing my parents a favor by looking after us. It seemed that Elrita and Joanne could get out of doing chores, but we couldn't. But I'm not sure my feelings were justified. I remember a night when I couldn't sleep. Uncle Hilmer let us all get out of bed, and he took us for a ride in the car, just for me. He knew how much I loved riding in the car."

The waning sunlight glistens on the blue-black lake. The rocking of the boat is my mother's cradling arms. The pflup, pflup of water slapping the side of the aluminum boat is her hand rhythmically patting my diapered bottom. Her voice is the drone of grown-ups talking in the living room as I fall asleep in my crib at night.

I shake my head clear as my mother continues her stories. Am I remembering or imagining my mother carrying me? Surely she lifted me from bassinet to changing table or playpen to shoulder. She took care of three children all day while my father worked; she must have carried us. I can't remember being transported by my mother's horsepower, yet this rocking boat vibrates an ancient chord.

With another shake of my head, I interrupt my reverie and Mom's nostalgia trip. "It's getting dark, Mom. We should head back to the dock."

Once inside, Mom urges me to find the video she's brought. It is a compilation of old family movies, transferred from 8mm film by her cousin Elrita's children. I press the play button, and Mom's memories are animated on the television screen. There are the matching sunsuits, the lake, and the rowboat. Aunt Elsie waves and smiles, four young girls run into the lake, perform an amateur synchronized swim, race, and laugh. My mother is vivacious, athletic, and energetic.

There is evidence of splicing as the girls in the film grow taller and grin at the camera. My mother runs sure-footed to the end of the dock and launches herself in a racer's dive that slices the water just below its surface. "We had an ongoing competition that summer, and I was the best diver," she narrates.

Christmas dinners and other family gatherings fill the gaps between summers at the lake. My mother and Elrita wave their diplomas at college graduation. Uncle Hilmer stands beside his prize roses. Suddenly we are back at Gages Lake, and my father appears in the film for the first time. He sits on the dock with his legs dangling in the water, smiling and handsome at age twenty-three. With a sharp intake of breath, I lean toward the TV, inhaling this image. The hollowness in my chest feels like hunger and breathlessness and heartache combined. The camera pans to my mother floating by his feet; her arms move in small circles, her legs, misshapen by polio, are made beautiful again by the rippling water.

As the scene shifts to the aunts and uncles walking toward the lake house, I relax in my chair, one eye on the screen and the other on my mother as she watches. A smile plays across her face, and she appears luminous. Her wrinkles and age spots, her gray hair and the tense set of her jaw are backlit by the energy of a younger Jane, a strong, smooth-cheeked girl who tossed her dark hair and giggled for the moviemaker.

For so long I have wanted my mother to be different—to love me more, to understand me, to take away my anger and sadness and want, and to love herself. I have been angry with her for her inability to change on my terms, and with myself for being selfish and heartless. Yet in this moment of seeing my mother as she was and is, and knowing what suffering has laid her low, my heart fills with love and an acceptance that in the past has appeared only in glimmers.

Chapter 8

Battling the Currents

February 1996

My time in Rochester is coming to an end, and my anxiety is rising. Although Jen and I planned to be with Mom from before the surgery to a week after discharge, we hadn't anticipated an advanced stage of cancer, a frightening prognosis, and a prolonged postoperative recovery. I will fly home to Philadelphia, leaving Mom making slow progress, her discharge date unknown, and her hospital stay already twice the average for bowel resection surgery. As an immediate solution, Jen takes another week off work, and I start to calculate when I can return.

When Jen arrives I am ready to go home but reluctant to let go. I recount my strategies in excruciating detail—how I've kept Mom afloat, focused her energies, steadied her emotions. I wonder how much of Mom's recuperation I've carried on my shoulders, with the stubborn determination she's teased me about since I was young. Can Jen keep Mom moving along the way I have? Can I let go of the idea that my way is the only way?

My trip to Philadelphia is slowed by bad weather, flight delays, and missed connections, but when I finally walk into the house, I revel in the rich colors of the stained-glass window in the front door, the dark cherry woodwork, the thick living-room carpet, the healthy pink of my children's faces, the warmth of my husband's embrace. It is soothing relief from the green surgical scrubs, mauve couches, pink walls, cold metal side rails, and snaking black cords connected to high-tech machinery that I've lived with for nearly two weeks. Yet as I try to reenter this full and vibrant life of mine, I am torn. A phone call at midday to check on Mom runs longer than expected, and I am late to a faculty meeting. An Internet search for articles to expand the literature review for the research grant I'm supposed to be working on degenerates into a surfing session through Web sites on colon cancer. I burn the onions and undercook the rice while booking next week's flight to Rochester. I drill the boys on their times tables, but forget to listen to the answers as I mull over Jen's latest report on Mom's progress. I read the words in the children's bedtime story, but in the back of my mind, I am setting goals for my next week with Mom. She is home on a Jell-O diet, and not yet ready to appreciate all the information I'm amassing on her behalf, so I practice on myself—I eat more vegetables, attend a support group for the families of cancer patients, and visualize the power of my immune system to fight off intruder cells.

It is almost a relief to return to Rochester on Sunday, where I can focus my full attention on Mom. Except that as soon as I board the plane, I miss the kids, and feel guilty for leaving them and for taking more time off work. There's no escaping feeling torn.

Mom seems tired and groggy when I arrive; her face is thinner than I expected. Telltale signs confirm Jen's report that she rarely leaves the couch and eats little. She wants to show me her pills; she's in pain, and wonders if it's time to take another. She assures me she's walked during the day—five steps from the couch to the commode and back again; she is eager to avoid my disapproval. She acknowledges that she hasn't made a decision about pursuing chemotherapy treatment for the cancer—the oncologist says it won't cure her, but can buy her some time.

I've been devouring information about cancer and its treatment, generating plans and hopes, and mustering resources for the next stage of Mom's recovery. But if I'm to be of any help to her, I need to trim my bloated expectations and adjust to her present reality.

The week passes quickly, and we make progress toward enabling Mom to manage at home on her own. She tackles the stair glide, and begins to sleep upstairs again. Her appetite improves, and trips to the bathroom become less traumatic. A routine develops around the visiting nurse who assesses her medical needs and manages her pain, the physical and occupational therapists who assign exercises to increase strength and create strategies for independent living, the home health aide who helps her bathe and dress, and the many friends who visit regularly, run errands, and bring meals. Her home is fitted with an emergency call system; she can summon help with a device worn around her neck.

I'm alert for indications that Mom is gearing up to manage on her own. She surprises me at the follow-up visit with the surgeon when she asks him when she'll be able to drive again. "As soon as you feel up to it, go ahead," he replies. Unable to censor his caustic wit, he adds, "Just let me know when you're venturing out on the roads so I can be sure to stay off them."

Despite that hint of interest in regaining independence, Mom continues to be clingy, cautious, passive, and fearful. On mornings when I leave her with the aide to run errands or just breathe in the outside world, she complains that I've been gone too long no matter how quickly I return. I remind her of the safeguards that we've put in place for emergencies, but her anxiety about being alone is palpable.

And so, week by week, we organize a tag team to stay with Mom. Barbara flies in from the same Montana town where she and Mom met thirty-nine years ago as young mothers and neighbors. She is a natural caregiver, and makes homemade soup, fills out Mom's tax forms, sorts her mail and medical bills, and laughs easily. Kevin, Tina, and Teija come from San Francisco to spend Easter with Mom. Several weeks later Mom's girlhood friend Natalie arrives from Chicago to stay for two weeks; they laugh and reminisce.

In between the longer visits from out-of-town friends, Mom cobbles together a schedule of local friends, using skills she's honed and relationships she's built in sixteen years of managing the day-care staff schedule. She asks for help without apology or a sense of entitlement—and people simply say yes.

I wonder how I would handle asking for help if I were in need.

My next trip to Rochester falls between Barbara and Natalie's visits, during my children's spring break from school so they can come too. I worry about juggling the needs of the kids, the dog, and my mother in her tiny house, so despite her pleas that we stay with her, I arrange accommodations at Connie's house, less than a mile away. Our time together will be easier if the children can escape their grandmother's pain and neediness each evening and she can take a break from their energy and youthful demands. After Kenwyn joins us midweek, I can stay with Mom alone. I explain my reasoning to Mom, and encourage her to spend those nights alone—a trial of independent living. "I'll be five minutes away. You can call me anytime," I reassure her.

But she lets me know that this is unthinkable; she hopes I'll relent and stay with her.

"Perhaps you could hire your health aide to stay overnight with you," I back off from pressuring her to look after herself, and she reluctantly makes arrangements with her aide.

When we arrive at Mom's house, her friend Mary Lou, who's been with her for the last few days, pulls me aside with a sense of urgency. "Your mother is not making much progress with walking and eating. And she's worried about your expectations. If you plan to go anywhere, you should get her a wheelchair right away. She nearly fell after her last visit to the oncologist—her legs just buckled beneath her as she walked." She tells me about a hospice where she sometimes works. "Maybe you should consider it for your mother."

"No," I think to myself. "Mom doesn't need hospice yet. She just needs to get some strength back and courage. She's got more time to enjoy!"

Mom lets the children turn on cartoons and calls for her pain medication. There is a new photograph of her next to the pill bottle. "My hairdresser came here last week. She did my hair and nails and makeup, too, then took this picture." At once striking and disturbing, the photo captures a gaunt beauty with sunken eyes and prominent cheekbones.

After dinner Mom's aide, Jaira, arrives, and I shuttle the children to Connie's house. I've just settled the kids in bed and am chatting with Connie when, at 11:30, the phone rings.

"Sara? I've fallen trying to go upstairs, and Jaira can't pick me up."

"Are you okay? How did you fall?"

"I didn't fall so much as I sank down. I didn't think Jaira could support my weight, and when I began to lose my balance, I just sank down. I didn't hurt anything, but I can't get back up."

I am annoyed and frustrated with Mom's inability to manage without me. I ask to speak with Jaira, hoping to come up with a strategy for how she can help Mom up on her own, but Mom calls out sharply, "Tell her she's going to have to come."

I am snippy as I stand in Mom's living room, arms crossed, barking instructions to Mom and Jaira. I offer little of my own strength so they'll understand just how easy it would have been to work this out without me. As soon as they are upstairs, I shout a quick good night and let myself out the front door.

In the morning, I am ready to consider Mary Lou's admonitions about Mom's mobility, and locate a medical equipment supply center to rent a wheelchair. After lunch we make our first excursion—a trip to the movies. We master the logistics of climbing in and out of the minivan and using the new wheelchair, but when we arrive at the theater, I discover that I've misread the movie schedule. *Muppet Treasure Island* doesn't begin for another hour and a half. We kill time at a nearby bookstore, and I worry about Mom's stamina, but she says she's up for going to the movies.

That evening, after our take-out pizza dinner, I glance around the living room at Mom, collapsed on the couch, and the children, engrossed in a video, and realize that we've each passed a test today. Mom has endured, if not completely enjoyed, a favorite activity; the children have tolerated Mom's special need of me; and I've carried several times my physical and emotional weight in my determination to make things appear normal. I don't ask if it's worth it; that would be much too complicated.

For the rest of the week, we alternate rest days with outings. After Kenwyn arrives we take our most ambitious trip, to Letchworth State Park, forty-five minutes outside of Rochester. The park offers dramatic views of cliffs and waterfalls as the river, swollen with the spring runoff of melting snow and ice, surges through a glacier-cut gorge. A brightly colored hot-air balloon prepares to take off from a field, and Kenwyn and the children enjoy a game of hide-and-seek. I watch to see if Mom is enjoying herself, but since we left home, she's been preoccupied with her untrustworthy intestinal system, embarrassed by her frequent and lengthy bathroom visits, and anxious. I don't want to admit that I've pushed her beyond her limits again. By the time we leave the park, the children are hungry and cranky and clamoring to stop at a restaurant. But we decide that Mom will be more comfortable at home, where I can prepare a quick meal while she rests. Despite how difficult the day has been for her, Mom is gracious. "This is the best food I've tasted since my surgery," she announces, finishing a plate of angel-hair pasta tossed with spinach, tomatoes, and blue cheese.

I don't want to be a bully, but left to her own devices, Mom is so passive. It's not that I think she's going to beat the cancer— but she can recover from the surgery, like the doctors have led us to expect, regain strength, decide about treatment, grapple with her feelings, and maybe have a few good months before the cancer ravages her. Everything I read, all the messages from the media and from society, suggest that the experience of living and dying with cancer can be richer, fuller, better if you have an open, active attitude.

Mom wants to hear about this kind of living with cancer—as long as I read the books. She thinks she'll give it a try—if I help. So I continue to show her what active living/dying might look like. When people suggest that I intimidate her, I wonder if they notice how carefully I listen, how hard I work to keep my expectations in line with her physical and emotional state.

She trusts me. She's just frightened.

But the next day, Mom's visiting nurse grabs me. "I'm worried about your mother. I don't think she can manage independently much longer. We may have to consider other options."

"Well, local friends are looking after her next week, then my sister and brother and their families are coming for Easter, and her girlhood friend a week or two later. I think we have things covered. Though if she's eligible for other supports that might help her stay at home . . ." My voice trails off with uncertainty, and the nurse jumps in with new ideas.

Neither the nurse nor I want to consider a hospice or a nursing home.

I keep close tabs on Mom over the next few weeks. When I call to wish the family a happy Easter, and Jen a happy birthday, I rattle off my standard questions, checking up on progress toward goals—my idea of progress toward my idea of goals, that is. "So, what outings have you all been on? How's Mom eating? Has she decided about the chemotherapy yet?"

"Well," Jen starts cautiously, "I don't think there have been any outings since you left. In fact, Mom doesn't even want to get out of her new electric lift chair. Last night she asked Kevin if he'd push her to the dinner table in it so she could join the family without getting up. 'It's this damn post-polio syndrome,' she keeps saying. She doesn't want to talk about the chemo. Dawn typed up everything the oncologist said when he laid out her options, but Mom hasn't looked at it since then."

At first I'm annoyed. Can't anyone besides me motivate Mom to get better enough to live the rest of her life, however short it is? But then I pause. Mom is living her life right now, enjoying being with Kevin and Jen and goofing off. They're giving her a gift by accepting her just as she is. Maybe I'm critical of how others are taking care of Mom because I'm jealous of their ability to relax and have fun together. It's not the first time I've felt outside the fun, absenting myself from it, judgmental of it, but at the same time wishing I were laughing, too.

During the next two weeks, Mom's energy level drops dramatically. The oncologist suggests a blood transfusion to give her a temporary boost, and asks if she's thought any more about treatment for the cancer. "Do I have to decide right away?" she asks again.

Mom is getting increasingly raggedy. I begin to doubt that she'll ever make enough gains—physically or psychologically—to live independently. When Natalie's two-week visit ends, she'll be back to the task of scheduling friends to stay with her night by night. She complains that it's becoming onerous; she feels like a burden. I circle the first week of May in my appointment book, and jot down "possible week in Rochester," but realize that Mom needs more than weeklong Band-Aids. Her anxiety about who will take care of her next is ruining her appetite, depleting her strength, and keeping her from facing the decisions she needs to make.

"Why don't you come down to Philadelphia and stay with us?" I offer gently. "If I come to visit you again, it can only be one week here, one week there. But if you come to my house, you can stay as long as you want. If you feel better, you can go home. If you're happy living with us, we'll all go to Long Lake at the end of June."

I want her to feel welcome, but not pressured. She may not be ready to think about never being able to cope on her own again.

"Oh, Long Lake," Mom sighs. "I can't think of a nicer place to be."

Without bothering to say yes, Mom jumps straight into the logistics, her voice revealing a deep sense of relief. "When should I come? How will I get there? Where will I stay? What will you do about work?"

I begin to make flight arrangements, but when I call Mom with options and details, she balks at the idea of flying alone. "Can't Jen drive to Rochester, fly with me to Philadelphia, fly back to Rochester, and then drive home to Albany?" she suggests. It seems to me an enormous hassle for Jen, just so Mom doesn't have to make the fifty-minute flight alone.

I wait until after Mom's blood transfusion to tell her the plans, hoping she'll feel more confident. "It will be fine, Mom. You can do this. Someone can take you to the airport, walk you onto the plane, and settle you in your seat. Sit tight for that one hour of flying, and I'll be there at the other end to help you off the plane."

Mom capitulates, but during the week, her friends repeat the worries that she can't say directly to me. "Sara is going to be surprised at how little I can do." "I'm afraid I'm going to be a disappointment to Sara." "I hope Sara realizes how much help I'm going to need."

"It doesn't matter to me what you can and can't do, Mom," I say the next time we talk. "I want you to come just the way you are."

I gather information about Mom's current energy level, sleep patterns, pain, and appetite to develop realistic expectations about her needs. Images begin to form: I'll settle her in a room outfitted with an intercom; she'll share in the evening meal, enjoy conversations with the children, and sit in the sunshine on the patio. Once she feels secure, we'll do her favorite things—go to the ballet and the movies, and visit with friends who have promised to come to Philadelphia. I'll create activities that Mom can enjoy with the children—a card game or looking at a scrapbook together. At the end of June, we'll take Mom to Long Lake. She'll be more debilitated by then, but what could be more peaceful than the lake, the mountains, the fresh summer breeze, and the sunsets?

"I'm worried about Mom," Jen says in a low, hurried voice from the upstairs phone in Mom's town house. "One of the first things she said to me when I got here to help her get ready to come to your house was, 'I can't believe how quickly the post-polio syndrome is progressing.' This is not post-polio syndrome! It's cancer! It drives me crazy when she talks about it that way. I feel like I'm in the twilight zone."

"She's not talking about cancer at all?" I am surprised.

"No," Jen says soberly.

"When is she going to make up her mind about chemotherapy?" I've spent hours organizing medical care for Mom in Philadelphia. Certain services can't be put in place until she makes a decision about treatment. "That's not all. The staff and parents of the day-care center wanted to honor her sixteen years of service and say good-bye before she leaves Rochester, but Mom refused a public event. She's let a few people visit her, but when they try to share what they feel about her and say good-bye, she puts up a wall and won't let the conversation get beyond the superficial."

Connie confirms Mom's withdrawal and denial; she suggests we challenge it. "Your mother never refers to the cancer; she's made post-polio syndrome the culprit. It's hindering her from doing the work she needs to do—sorting out her affairs, saying good-byes, taking care of unfinished emotional business. I can't imagine what it will be like for you to take care of her if she continues to put off dealing with the fact that she is dying of cancer." For years Connie has helped Mom think through decisions, handle conflicts, express her feelings, and confront her blind spots. After they talk Connie recounts their conversation to me.

"You're going to have to stop thinking about this as post-polio syndrome. You have to name it, to talk about the cancer," Connie suggests to Mom.

"I haven't wanted to talk about it because I know I have to fight it, and I guess I'm not ready."

"Well, it depends on what you mean by fighting it. You can fight to make your last days what you want them to be instead of fighting to make them last another month. Do some of the things that you want to do before you die: spend time with your children, grandchildren, and friends; say the things you want to say to people."

"You talk as if I don't have much time."

"That's right. You have cancer, and you don't have much time."

"How much time? A year?"

"I'm afraid we're talking about months, not a year."

"I've been so afraid of this. I haven't wanted to know." The tears begin to spill.

But by the next day, Mom's clarity reverts to cloudiness. "Connie came over last night, and we had an important discussion," she says to Jen. "Maybe she'll come again tonight so you can hear it, too."

That evening the three of them go over it again.

"There's stuff I just haven't wanted to know. But I guess I should hear it all. Go ahead and tell me everything."

"There's nothing you don't know," Connie and Jen protest.

"Then why don't you tell it to me again."

"How about if you tell us what you know, and we'll fill in anything you leave out," Connie suggests.

"Okay. I have cancer of the colon. It has perforated the intestinal wall and spread to my liver." She looks at Jen and Connie expectantly.

"That's it," they reply. "You know it all."

She looks at her lap, her fingers weaving nervously.

"What is most frightening to you about dying," Connie asks gently after a few moments of silence. "Is it about not being anymore?"

"No, I don't think I'm as afraid of being dead as I am of dying. Pain. Being alone. Losing control. Those things."

That night as Jen helps Mom into bed, she says peevishly: "I don't care what you and Connie say. It's the post-polio syndrome that bothers me the most."

Chapter 9
Climbing off the Fence

May 1996

I wiggle my feet absently, tangling myself in the sheets of my makeshift bed, unable to fall asleep. A mental tape is stuck on continuous play reviewing the day's events. It begins at the airport, where passengers stream through the jetway and I beg the airline attendant to let me board the plane to escort my mother, as I had promised I would. I am told that it is against airline policy, and instructed to wait. "We will bring your mother to you," the attendant says with confidence.

I win the battle to board the plane at last—not by my negotiation skills but by my mother's refusal to let the stewards move her without me. One of them relents, finds me still arguing my case, and brings me to my mother. She is surrounded by a huddle of flight attendants and a plane full of empty seats. Her eyes are wide and still, like a deer caught in the headlights of a car, and they flood with tears as I bend to hug her.

We have taken so long to disembark that Mom's two blue suitcases sit alone beside the empty luggage carrousel, clattering along its track. I roll her wheelchair in line with the chairs in the waiting area, murmur, "You'll be fine here; I'll be right back," then run the equivalent of two city blocks to long-term parking lot C. To get to passenger pickup, I must circle the airport in the minivan, finally pulling up at the curb in front of the No Parking sign. I beg the indulgence of the security guard, whose hand is poised above a ticket pad, and push through the revolving door to find my mother, her eyes anxiously glued on the entrance. The security guard catches sight of us as I push the wheelchair up the ramp toward the car, and he is transformed from the officious enforcer of the rules to an ambassador of the city. He offers to lift my mother into the car; he smiles at her and jokes lightly.

At home Kenwyn gently helps Mom from the car and begins to roll the wheelchair toward the back door. It jerks and shudders over the cracks in the sidewalk, the gravel-coated driveway, the uneven patio bricks, and the five-inch threshold into the house. I cringe at these obstacles that I've never noticed before as my mother's hands grip her armrests.

Justin, Phillip, and Kalila greet their grandmother from a distance, moving closer only when they feel the pressure of my hand in the small of their backs. They lean away from her forced smile of normalcy, alert to the illness and fear that it masks, then dart toward and away again, weaving a tangled May dance before retreating to the familiarity of the backyard swing set.

I show Mom the room I've prepared. Grandma Corse's Canadian maple-leaf quilt covers the bed and colorful artwork hangs on the wall—one masterpiece donated by each child. There is a rocking chair on one side of the bed and a couch on the other. The large closet is empty and waiting, the bathroom is wheelchair accessible, and the adjacent room holds a couch that can double as a bed for visitors. I'm pleased with what I've done with the space, and hope that Mom will be, too.

We unpack the suitcases, and I arrange nightgowns, sundresses, and sweat suits on the shelves. The bag of adult diapers in her suitcase embarrasses her. "I can't believe I've been reduced to this," she says. "I didn't think I'd be able to make it here on the plane without them, but I did."

In the midst of settling in, Mary Ellen, a young teacher and friend from the day-care center, drives up to the house in

Mom's car. It is filled to the brim with a TV and VCR, extra pillows, picture albums and scrapbooks, books, and framed photographs—items culled from a household, a lifetime—the bare essentials. Mary Ellen will fly back to Rochester tomorrow, leaving the car with us for doctor's appointments, outings, or emergencies.

Mary Ellen is cheerful and joking in Mom's presence, but when we are alone, she bursts into tears. "I just don't know how I'm going to get along without her. She's helped me through so much in the last couple of years." This is not the first friend of Mom's to express that sentiment—not the first young woman who has been like a daughter to my mother.

When we are finished unpacking, Kenwyn wheels Mom to the living room, grunting with exertion as he tilts the chair onto its back wheels and forces them over the ledge, bouncing and bumping. We awkwardly transfer her from wheelchair to couch, search for the right combination and position of pillows and move an end table nearby to hold the little tote basket she fills with medications, lotion, lip cream, tissues, and whatever book she wishes she could be reading.

She is tired. "What station is the comedy channel here in Philadelphia? I may fall asleep, but I seem to need the TV on for distraction."

I leave Mary Ellen and Mom in the company of the cast of *Politically Incorrect,* and prepare dinner. As I call everyone to the table, only ten minutes later than planned, I am pleased to have carried on with the normal family schedule. But my timing is off. Mom needs to use the commode, which is a bumpy wheelchair ride back to the bedroom. By the time we've solved that problem and I've wheeled Mom to her place at the table, the family is asking for second helpings. She shakes her head when she sees the meal I've prepared. "I'm sorry, Sara, but I don't think I can chew or swallow anything like this. Do you have any soup?" Fortunately there is a small convenience store across the street from our house, and I find a can of Campbell's Chunky Style Chicken Vegetable Soup. I must run it through the blender twice before Mom can force any of it down her throat. She eats a scant quarter of a cup, though it takes her until long after everyone else has been excused from the table. I remember when I was six or seven years old—Mom kept me company at the dining-room table many evenings while I finished my dinner. She'd sit and read the newspaper and repeat some variant of "you're slower than molasses in January."

I ask Mom at ten o'clock and again at eleven if she's tired and ready for bed; I certainly am. She relents after the local news, and we embark on our first run-through of the bedtime routine. The wheelchair fits snugly under the sink in the bathroom, and though Mom lacks the strength to squeeze out the washcloth, she methodically washes her face, applies Pond's Night Moisturizing Cream, and brushes her teeth.

I stand nearby ready to help, watching her in the mirror. She looks beautiful to me—the blaze in her eyes and the curve of her cheekbone.

When she is settled in bed, I pull the covers to her shoulders, kiss her, and say, "I love you, Mom."

"I love you, too, sweetie. And thank you."

For years "I love you, Mommy" stuck in my throat, threatening to betray my ambivalence and my need. Now the words are easy and honest. Without conscious effort, without sorting through feelings or discussing issues, Mom and I are forgiving each other our inadequacies in loving; perhaps we are forgiving ourselves.

Today has been momentous, with miscalculations, logistical nightmares, and moments of suffering, but also miraculous— filled with a spirit of tender love.

My breathing slows, and I relax toward sleep.

"Sara? Sara!" My mother's weak but persistent call invades my light dream. I must have drifted off at last.

"What is it, Mom?" I call back, though I know I have to leave this cozy bed and go to her.

"I need to turn over. I can't move by myself."

I slog into her room and turn on the bedside lamp. Mom looks at me apologetically, expecting my irritation. But I am not annoyed, just groggy and sad and wishing I could ease her pain. I know how to brush away her apology with a cheery bedside-nurse greeting, having noted the best techniques during Mom's hospitalization.

"My back is killing me, and I can't turn over in this bed."

"Okay, I'll help." Mom is relaxed by my tone of voice.

She grasps my hand so I can pull her onto her side; her gaunt shoulders and arms are surprisingly strong. But she is unable to shift her hips, and begins to roll back. I run around the bed to push from behind and ease her top leg over for balance.

"Use that little gold pillow I brought, the one Grandma Klein kept in her living room. I call it Squish. Where's Squish?" Mom asks. She sounds like a young child, though she hasn't lost her wits. She's just frightened.

I retrieve the velvet pillow from under the covers and wedge it against her back to keep her from rolling. "Are you all right now?" I can't help myself from inclining in the direction of my bed as I say this, countering the pull of her wish for me to linger. She sighs and nods, releasing the tension that holds me there.

I nestle back into bed and try to shake the image of my mother's emaciated upper body, the unnatural swelling in her legs and belly.

Mom calls again after I've dropped into deep sleep, and I find it more difficult to rouse myself. This time she needs help to use the commode. She worries that I'll hurt myself lifting her from the bed to the seat, but I'm beginning to learn how to position the commode and make use of the dynamics of heft and swing. She tugs ineffectually at her nightgown as it rides up, and I keep my eyes averted. Then it's back to bed with Squish and another kiss.

She calls once more before dawn.

I droop back to bed, worried that I won't have the stamina to care for Mom, run the household, and look after the children if I am awakened this many times each night.

When I wake in the morning, Mom is still sleeping, so I leave her to check on the family's preparations for church. The children are reluctant to hurry, and lobby to stay home when they find out that I'm not going. But Kenwyn shuttles them out the door.

An hour later I peer around the doorjamb to Mom's room; she's wide awake, eager to use the commode, and irked that I've left her alone with no way of getting my attention. I encourage Mom to do the exercises her physical therapist taught her; I am eager to establish a sense of routine. She flings five-pound hand weights around with surprising ease. "Let's skip the bath," she says when she sees me frowning at the bathroom door, considering logistics. "I was perfectly clean when I left Rochester, and I can't have gotten too dirty yet."

I help her dress, and then position the wheelchair close to the bed. We are both nervous as I bend my knees, place my arms around her chest, and lift. She is fully reliant on my strength to move her into the chair. I wheel her outside and settle her on the patio with some applesauce and cottage cheese. We chat while I pull out the tiny Norway maple shoots sprouting in my neglected garden. Later I convince Mom to tour the neighborhood. "There are beautiful rock gardens in front of a set of row houses in the next block, just bursting with flowers. It's my favorite spot in the neighborhood these days." But the wheelchair bumps erratically along the brick sidewalks, and Mom, though politely attentive, tires quickly.

While Mom dozes on the couch with the TV on, I bustle around the house, putting things away and cleaning, my mind racing. Wherever I go, projects that have been steadily accumulating over the years of full-time work and motherhood call out to me. There are drawers and closets to organize, silver to polish, woodwork to paint, clothes to mend, a dog to walk, and plants to tend. Shouldn't I tackle some of those while I'm taking time off work to care for Mom? Never mind special projects; will I be able to keep up with the basic housework and give the children what they need so my mother's situation doesn't dominate the scene? And what about Mom? Her legs are swollen, her appetite tiny, her back throbbing, her nights restless. She's unable to walk or stand or shift her weight; she's in pain. Will I make it until her oncology appointment and the setting up of hospice services? Will it get any easier? Can I give her what she needs for as long as she needs?

I'm having trouble working out a way for Mom to call me when I'm somewhere else in the house or yard, or sleeping in my own bed. Phillip's souvenir Liberty Bell gives a faint tinny jangle, but not enough to get my attention even when I'm only in the next room. The intercom system doesn't work with our configuration of phone and electrical lines. I rigged up the two phone lines, but Mom says that she can't see what two buttons she needs to press. She's not making it easy, but I keep trying. I really want to get back to my own bed at night.

"Sara," Mom calls in a shaky voice. "I need to ask you about tonight."

"What about tonight?"

"Well, I find myself worrying all day long, waiting for you to tell me whether you're going to sleep in the room next to mine or upstairs. I can't stand the suspense anymore. Can you please tell me now so I can get used to the idea?"

"Don't worry, Mom. I won't spring anything on you at the last minute. I'll only sleep in my room if we come up with a system that we test beforehand and know will work perfectly for you."

She's terrified of being alone.

"She seems worse than when she was in Rochester," I tell Jen when she calls. "I thought she'd improve knowing that she had me to take care of her."

Mom and I are anxious before her first appointment with the oncologist at the University of Pennsylvania Cancer Center. It takes all morning to get Mom dressed, medicated, fed, and into the front seat of the minivan. I load the wheelchair in the back and drive the few blocks to the center. Can Mom tell that I'm putting up a front of competence so she won't be anxious? Is she as worried as I am that the wheelchair will roll away or slip from under her as I lower her from the car?

We wait in several lines, complete various forms, and thumb through magazines in the waiting room before the oncologist is ready to see Mom. He looks young. I hope he knows what he's doing.

"What a nice sweatshirt," he says to Mom with genuine caring. "I love lighthouses, too. I did my residency in Boston."

He follows with a few medical questions in a kindly and nonthreatening manner.

"I know I should be eating more," Mom volunteers as he listens to her breathing.

"That's not your fault," he replies. "Your loss of appetite is caused by the cancer."

Mom asks him about treatment options, and he describes the same protocols and side effects that we've heard before.

"It's hard for me to get to the bathroom. Does everyone experience diarrhea?"

"It's fairly typical."

"Well, do I have to decide right away?"

Here is the same question Mom has asked the oncologists since her surgery ten weeks earlier. How much time does she think she has?

The oncologist turns to me before we leave. "Cancer is a family issue. Given that your mother and grandfather were stricken with colon cancer in their early sixties, you aren't at greater risk for the early-onset variety that appears in the forties or fifties. But by the time you reach your forties, you should have regular screenings. When detected early it can often be treated successfully."

It is frightening, but comforting, to hear my fears spoken aloud.

In trying to get Mom home after the doctor's appointment, we are both shaken when her legs fold beneath her while getting out of the car, and she lands on the sidewalk instead of the wheelchair. A neighbor walking past with his dog helps me lift Mom. She is relieved to get inside and collapse on the couch.

Mom may not have the energy, but we need to talk. If she doesn't make a decision about treatment soon, it'll be too late. And because in Pennsylvania, a patient is eligible for hospice services only if he or she has less than six months to live and has decided not to pursue treatment to eradicate the disease, we can't activate all the services she needs in order to be cared for at home until she decides. I let her rest until just before the kids are due home from school, then plop down beside her.

"What have you been thinking about?"

"Well, about the decision I'm supposed to make."

"Which decision?" I want her to say it on her own.

"About the chemotherapy."

"Well, what do you think about it?" I know what I think. For weeks I've been rehashing the postoperative report, researching proposed treatments, working the odds ratios, trying to make it come out different. Certain words and numbers won't go away. Incurable. Six-month life expectancy without treatment. Twenty percent chance of buying a few months. Side effects of nausea, diarrhea. No matter how I arrange the data, it adds up to more suffering with little potential gain. But I want to know what she's been thinking.

"I don't think I can handle having diarrhea for several days each week. I don't want you to have to lift me on and off the commode all day." We talk about side effects for a few minutes, stopping when we hear the children clomp up the front porch steps.

Later that afternoon I bring it up again. "Have you thought more about what you want to do?"

"Well, it depends on whether you're asking me what I want to do or what I think I should do."

"Tell me what you want to do."

"I don't want to do the chemotherapy, but I think I should."

"Why should you?"

"I should fight the cancer. I shouldn't let people down."

"Who are you worried about letting down?" I ask. "You won't be letting me down, or Kevin or Jen or Connie. We've all talked about it. It's okay with us if you don't do the chemo."

I think that will ease her mind, but it doesn't. She closes her eyes and sighs.

"Who are you worried about letting down?" I ask again; there is a long silence.

"My mother."

Her mother's been dead for over ten years.

"Why would that let your mother down?"

"She would expect me to fight, like she expected me to learn to walk again after the polio. But I don't know if I have another fight left in me."

Did my grandmother struggle, as I do, about when to stand back and accept her daughter's limits and when to push harder? Did she hope when her daughter despaired? Did she rush to help or force herself to stand back while her daughter labored up the steps to the apartment in orthopedic shoes, leg braces, and crutches? Did she give away her daughter's high-heeled shoes, danced in at college balls and sorority parties, or keep them in the back of a closet just in case?

And how did my mother feel about her mother's way of helping? Was she grateful or resentful? When her mother asked her to "Try a little harder. Stand on your tiptoes," was she angry about the unrealistic demand, or humiliated that she could not deliver the full recovery her mother hoped for?

"How are you feeling about our conversation?" I ask Mom after dinner.

"I don't know. I shouldn't just give up."

"Mom, deciding not to do the chemotherapy isn't giving up.

It's choosing a different kind of fight. If you do the chemo, you'll begin each week worrying about the next appointment: how you'll manage the trip to the doctor, the blood tests, the treatment, the aftereffects. You'll wonder when the diarrhea will hit, how you'll cope. If you're lucky you'll have one or two days each week when you're not preoccupied.

"If you elect not to do chemo, you can use your energy for other things, like spending time with the children or calling a friend. We can go for a walk or sit outside and listen to the birds. We can go to a movie or just talk. Those choices are just as honorable; they require just as much fight as chemotherapy."

Mom blows her nose, smiles weakly, and nods.

Interlude II

Leap of Faith

". . . you ride on the wings of the wind."
—*Psalm 104:3*

February 1998

I struggle to find my center while spinning, fight inner demons to claim my space on the ice for practicing, and battle the force of gravity and the fear of falling when jumping. To become airborne is a leap of faith that entails first bending deep for a sense of firm grounding, then letting go in controlled explosion. I wonder often, and with every jump I attempt, if I will ever conquer the doubt and fear that bind me so firmly to earth.

The bunny hop is an easy introduction to jumping—a skip or a hop on ice; the skater is in the air for just a moment while still moving forward. The greatest risk is tripping on the toe pick and falling forward. Seems innocuous, but it is enough to bring my heart into my throat.

The waltz jump introduces the skater to the sensation of springing up and turning in the air. The skater takes off on a forward outside edge and rotates 180 degrees before landing on the opposite foot skating backward. By bending the knee, lowering the arms, and holding the torso steady in a lunge, the skater lowers her center of gravity, increasing the potential force applied to the ice at takeoff. From this position, on a curving edge that begins the half-rotation, the leg forcefully extends, the arms accelerate upward in the direction of the jump, and the trunk is held stable, projecting the skater into the air. Landing with a soft bend in the knee settles the skater back onto the ice.

I discover every possible way to dissipate the energy necessary for a proper waltz jump. Lacking strength, balance, and confidence in the early days of skating, I bend only slightly in the knee and limit the force compressed in the skating leg. Having created little power to spring into the air, I barely leave the ice before I have landed. Body alignment and stability are also essential for creating energy for the jump. When the on-ice rotation is held in check, the back and shoulders and hips preserve power for leaping and rotating. This stillness, this powerful check, requires balance and control and courage. When I can't hold the check, I open out before leaving the ice, killing the momentum.

To ride on the wings of the wind, you first need to connect firmly with the earth. Though the skate blade etches a shallow trough in the ice and is continuously moving, I deepen my connection by envisioning long roots anchoring me in the ground.

After my father died, the family felt rootless. We assured Mom that we were still whole, that it wasn't only Dad or even primarily Dad who created for us a sense of family. But, in fact, he was the rock—silent, solid, ancient, of the earth.

The Corse family and its various branches came to America in the 1700s from Scotland and France and England, to settle in the farming areas of Vermont, New Hampshire, and northern New York. My grandmother traced her ancestry to settlers who fought in the Revolutionary War. My father's family began as farmers, then produced builders and forest rangers—a place-bound clan, rooted in the earth.

My mother's family immigrated later, uprooted from cities and towns in Northern and Eastern Europe and repotted, not in the rural Northeast but in the urban Midwest. City plants send out roots tenacious enough to break through concrete; they grow leaves with greater capacity to convert carbon dioxide to oxygen than do their rural counterparts. My mother's parents were assimilated survivors. Making their way in the city during the Depression, they lived in apartments and never owned a house, much less acres of land. Nor were they spiritually rooted—Leo, a Jew disinterested in religion, and Inez, a sometimes Presbyterian. Instead they were inquisitive, cynical, and pragmatic—not rooted in a sense of place or religious heritage, but bound together by a web of relationships.

My mother was attracted to the solidity of my father's history at the same time that she disparaged the small-town narrow-mindedness she sensed in her visits to Sandy Creek. Still, she craved the distance from her family that marriage provided. She was all too ready to escape from her mother's painful blend of overprotectiveness and denial of her limitations after polio. She was weary of her father's alternating aloofness and biting sarcasm.

As a child I was more connected with the Corse family than the Klein family. After the family moved to Sandy Creek, I saw the Corses more often, heard the family stories, visited the places, and met the faces that filled their lives. I was deeply familiar with their manner of speaking and preferences for food, their rhythms, and their smells. My father's decision to move back east to be near his family after his father died reinforced the sense of Corse family solidity. It made Dad solid. It made us all solid.

Or so it appeared to me. I didn't see the cracks then.

Then he died, and my mother crumbled.

My sister and brother and I pretended that our family had not fallen apart, for Mom's sake at least, but we crumbled, too. We lived amid the rubble.

I think about this now as I skate. Lurching takeoffs, incomplete revolutions, and faltering landings seem more consistent with my way of being in the world than flowing edges, powerful spring in the knees, and perfect timing. I wonder if my indecision, my fear of taking risks, of falling, would be less today if the rug hadn't being pulled out from under the family when Dad died—if I hadn't internalized my mother's anxiety and insecurity along with a sense of responsibility for alleviating it. If I had known the support of a father at age twenty-one when I was deciding my career direction, twenty-six when I married, twenty-nine when I first gave birth—even now as I write this— would I feel more grounded, courageous, decisive? Would I be able to take a leap of faith?

Legs straight, skittering along the surface of the ice, the skater does not get enough purchase to jump very high.

She has to dig in.

And yet not so much that she gets stuck.

Can any of us count on our parents to keep us grounded and rooted? When parents die before their children are grown? When parents haven't grown up themselves? When they are struggling to make ends meet or create meaning in their own lives, or just trying to feel okay about each day? I can't blame my fear of leaping on my father. And yet after his death, I know I kept one foot on the ground out of trepidation and a sense of duty. Even as I vigorously strove to extricate myself from my mother's psychic pain, I tethered myself to the space around her . . . just in case. I didn't want to bear the consequences of sailing away—of surpassing her.

"I had a dream last night, very disturbing," Mom said the day after Christmas 1983. Kenwyn and I were visiting for our first Christmas with my family. "I dreamt that I was looking in my closet for a dress to wear to a party. Your father was alive. I reached for a beautiful black dress, but when I lifted the hanger and pulled the dress out of the closet, it was very heavy. I looked down and saw leg braces attached to the dress." She burst into tears.

I was a psychologist-in-training. My mother was not safe with me.

"Don't you sometimes feel angry at Dad," I honed in. It had been six years since his death.

"All the time," Mom replied. "I'm furious at him for dying on me."

"That's not exactly what I meant," I said without hesitation. "I was wondering if you felt angry at him for making it possible for you to live all those years without having to work through your feelings about being handicapped—in a way he robbed you of the experience of finding your own way."

"I don't know what you mean," she replied in a curt, dismissive tone, "I am angry at him for dying, that's all."

My father dead. A black dress. No more parties. Leg braces. Tears. Maybe it was presumptuous of me to analyze my mother's dream that way, but it made sense to me—how my mother couldn't seem to let go, move on, or grow up, how I was tied to her.

Did those braces represent something about me, too? Bound but not rooted; unable to separate but unwilling to stay. Afraid to take the leap.

The toe loop is the first "real jump" a skater learns. It is a three-quarter rotation accomplished by jabbing the ice with the toe pick and pole-vaulting into the takeoff; horizontal motion is abruptly transferred to vertical lift. I develop an aversion to jabbing the ice. I tell myself, "Do it, just do it. Stab the ice with your toe pick." But at the last moment, I go weak in the calf and ankle, and my knee turns to jelly.

The salchow is a jump off the back inside edge. The body alignment must shift subtly, along with the pressure on the blade. I struggle with this jump as well, leaning just a little too far forward and scraping my toe pick noisily along the ice before take-off. It is an effective braking system, and I land as if on a dime, with no flow into my next move.

The loop jump has been eluding me for months as well—a full-rotation jump off the back outside edge to land on the same foot. Though I've been skating backward for a few years now, the body alignment, the lean into the center, still feels foreign. I rarely fall—I won't let myself if I can help it—but when I do, it is usually while skating backward. I have hit my head, landed on my knee, banged my elbow, jabbed my shin with a skate blade, and bruised my hip, all more than once. "I should spend an entire year skating only backward. Maybe that would help."

All jumping involves letting go, allowing forward and upward momentum to build to completion, creating a wave of motion and riding it to its peak. Once the skater crests, gravity takes over and there is no ambiguity about the return to earth. Still I can't let go of that worry. I cheat the going up because I'm already concerned with the coming down. Kalila takes lessons, too, and when we practice together, my struggle is visible to her. "Don't jump *down*, Mom, jump *up!*" she laughs.

I try. But the truth is, I am afraid. Being afraid for the future, only a split second away, I can't stay faithful to the present. If I could let go of that fear, if I could stay with the here and now, I would discover something wonderful between the taking off and the landing—I would know how it feels to fly.

To be available to the transforming power of the present moment and to ground myself deeply in the source of light and love, the eternal divine, I must let go of the image of myself as victim—bereaved, heart-wounded, orphaned. To grow too comfortable with grief and sadness, with a sense of loss and "poor me" is to veer off the path of love. The wounded healer is not the same as the walking wounded.

And yet I needn't banish tears—there is a place for sorrow. Perhaps the essence of God's gift of the wounded healer is to teach us that we can't separate the depths from the heights.

I write "Dear God" letters in my journal, praying, "Help me to operate not out of the sense that I have been abandoned by others, but out of the faith that I have not been abandoned by you."

Occasionally someone watching me skate in a practice session will comment on what a lovely skater I am, how graceful I look. I don't quite believe them—it doesn't feel that way on the inside. Instead I measure myself against a higher standard: "Jump higher. Kick your foot to the ceiling. Check harder. Grab the energy and pull."

I wonder if I hold back because I am afraid of the heights I might reach if I were to dig down to the depths to which I am capable of going. And yet I yearn for that greater rootedness in God, the source of the love we seek from one another, the wellspring. "Draw me to that silent center, hold me in the palm of your hand, and at the same time, free me, release me, make me a wild, creative expression of your love."

Chapter 10

Letting Go

May 1996

The hospice nurse, Tracy, comes to the house to initiate home health services. She asks Mom if she understands that hospice is for people in their last months of life; it is palliative care, not treatment of disease. Mom calmly reiterates her decision not to be treated for the cancer; her tone is sure. And though I believe in the integrity of her choice, my heart catches in my throat, and I turn quickly to wipe my tears before they are seen.

Tracy assesses Mom's level of pain from tumors pressing against her spine and organs, her nutritional status, her need for help in getting around and taking care of herself. "I'll be visiting at least twice a week," she explains, "and we can arrange for an aide to come in the morning for bathing, dressing, and changing bed linens. I'm going to ask the doctor to prescribe a morphine patch. It will be more effective than the oral painkillers. You might want to pick up the first prescription to get it started; then you can ask for home delivery."

The next day the social worker evaluates Mom's emotional adjustment, our resources for caring, and the likely impact it will have on the family. She comments on Mom's quiet courage, her insistence on rising each morning, exercising, washing, dressing, and moving from bed to couch for the day. She notes our relationship, and how we've set things up for Mom. "Most of the patients I see have taken to their beds, are withdrawn or bitter or irritable. Many of the families have great difficulty coping," she points out to us.

I'm pleased but worried. Though we appear to be handling things well, I'm already feeling the strain of getting up many times a night and responding to Mom's fear of being alone. "In Rochester Mom's aide came for four hours each morning, and the medical system was poised to offer her help at night. Can't we have more than one or two hours of help a day?"

"The aide will only provide for your mother's immediate physical needs, not her laundry or cooking or housework since you are here. And no, we don't provide night nursing aides. You'll have to hire someone privately. I can ask the volunteer coordinator to find someone to stay with your mother while you collect the children from school or run errands," the social worker explains.

I guess I'm going to be on duty twenty-four hours a day.

"And how about if I send the chaplain to see you. He's a Lutheran, very gentle and understanding. Would you like him to visit?"

I look to Mom for a response, and she surprises me with a yes.

"Good," says the social worker as she gathers her papers to leave. "You are both doing a great job."

"Thanks for the vote of confidence," I say, but I'm not sure I can keep up the heroics.

Mom is worried about the same thing. "I don't like to disturb you at night. Sometimes I lie awake for many minutes before I call you. I know it doesn't make any sense, because I eventually do have to wake you up. But I wait, as if giving you a few more minutes to sleep is less disruptive. Why don't you find someone to help you?"

"I will. It's crazy for you to feel guilty about calling me for help in the night." I flash to an image of myself at the age of eight, glued to the top step of the stairs, afraid of the creak that will alert Mom and Dad to my sleeplessness.

After several phone calls yield several no's, I find an agency prepared to send us an aide right away. "I hope this person will be able to lift me. I hope she'll hear me when I call. I hope she'll be nice," Mom nervously responds to the news.

That night I orient the new aide, extricate myself from Mom's anxiety, and enjoy a full night's sleep.

The next day I tackle the problem with Mom's vision. Since the surgery Mom has complained that she can't focus well enough to read. "I don't know if it's my glasses or my concentration, but I miss reading. I wish I could use it to distract myself."

I call a local optometrist, and once I explain Mom's situation, an appointment miraculously opens up in what I'd been told was a full schedule. The office is five blocks away, and though the way is bumpy, Kenwyn rolls Mom there in her wheelchair to avoid the awkward transfers in and out of the car. Within a few days, Mom's new glasses are ready. The assistant offers to hand deliver them and adjust them on the spot. The glasses are attractive. I've never known Mom to choose such expensive frames, though, or write a check of that size with no comment.

Over the next few days, Mom puts her glasses on several times and tries to read. But by the end of the week, she has given up; they settle to the bottom of her tote basket, hidden beneath tissues and tubes of ointment.

Mom seems more relaxed now that we have a routine established and extra help. But she isn't gaining strength, energy, appetite, an interest in getting out, or the ability to sleep through the night— none of the improvements I'd hoped would come after her move to Philadelphia. I'm beginning to suspect that she never will— that while she appeared to be more functional in Rochester, she really was just holding on by the skin of her teeth, sustained through the moving preparations and the trip to Philadelphia by a mixture of adrenaline, anxiety, and determination. Now that she's here and feels safe, now that she no longer faces decisions about treatment or worries about who will take care of her next, she can let go.

I need to let go, too. It's not something I'm good at.

March 1977

In the weeks after Dad's death, I seek out the poem read by one of our minister friends at the funeral. "Wild Grapes," by Robert Frost (1920), is a story-poem about a little girl and her older brother, who gather grapes from a fruit-laden vine that has entwined itself around a birch tree. The girl cannot reach the grapes, and she is too small to climb up a tree, so her brother first throws grapes down to her. Then, to enable independent picking, he bends the supple birch to within her reach, and instructs:

> "Here, take a treetop, I'll get down another.
> Hold on with all your might when I let go."

The young girl proves to be a mighty holder; once released by the brother, the supple tree sails to upright, its new fruit still clinging. The boy cries out to his sister: "Let go! Don't you know anything, you girl? Let go!" but she, descended of monkeys, can't let go. She hangs on while her brother coaxes, cajoles, demands, and threatens, until finally he thinks to bend the tree again and set her on the ground. He chastises her for not weighing anything.

> It wasn't my not weighing anything
> So much as my not knowing anything—
> My brother had been nearer right before.
> I had not taken the first step in knowledge;
> I had not learned to let go with the hands,
> As still I have not learned to with the heart,
> And have no wish to with the heart—nor need,
> That I can see. The mind—is not the heart.
> I may yet live, as I know others live,
> To wish in vain to let go with the mind—
> Of cares, at night, to sleep; but nothing tells me
> That I need learn to let go with the heart.

This poem comforts me; I am no more able to let go with the heart than is its narrator. Grief for my father reminds me that I am real, that I feel. The young men who win my heart after his death, the friends I let close, are those that sense the sadness shadowing my cheerfulness and enthusiasm, and understand the hysterical edge to my laughter.

Healing from loss may be about getting on with life, but it can't be about letting go.

Slowly I am letting go of my insistence that Mom try to get out and do things. She shows no interest in going to the movies, the theater, the ballet, or shopping, so I stop thinking about getting her out of the house. She no longer tries to read. She doesn't even want to use the audiotape and book that the volunteer brought her from the library.

She asks for a video every night, and she's doing her best to engage with the kids for a few minutes each day. One day I organize a going-away party for Mandy, a student at the University of Pennsylvania who takes care of Justin, Phillip, and Kalila after school. We sit on the living-room floor, incorporating Mom into our circle. We have a snack, and I ask each child to tell Mandy what they've enjoyed about their time with her. "The pictures you draw!" they all shout. Mom stays alert and watches with interest.

A few days later, Justin is home from school with a cold. I settle him in the living room with Mom, and try to juggle their different needs. "Can I watch cartoons?" Justin asks plaintively, after putting up with an hour of *Politically Incorrect* reruns. "Oh, please. Not some animated superhero show," Mom warns. After coming up with several options that result in a veto from one or the other, I find a family video that begins with the twins' first day home from the hospital. Finally both Mom and Justin are happy as they watch first smiles, first steps, and first words.

One day a friend offers to stay with Mom while I go shopping. Mom is nervous about being left with a stranger—she asks two or three times how long I plan to be gone. Becca assures

Mom that she can handle anything that might arise, reminding her that she is a nurse.

As I sort through the racks of dresses at the department store, looking for a dress for an upcoming wedding, I notice myself choosing with my mother's preferences in mind.

Pulling a long dress over my head in the fitting room and watching in the mirror as its flowing black skirt swirls around my shins before settling above my ankles, I think, "Mom will love this dress."

I'm still wearing the suits and dresses that Mom and I chose seven years ago when we braved the after-Christmas-sales crowd to bargain hunt for my "professional wardrobe." Mom sat on a chair outside each dressing room while I modeled. She was effusive, admiring, and proud; I felt beautiful. That day she didn't steal my pleasure by complaining about her own reflection in the mirror or blocking her view of herself with a raised hand. She didn't ask if she was as fat as the lady at the checkout counter or repeat that she planned to never wear a dress or show her legs again. She didn't remind me of the comment I made before leaving for graduate school, when I was envisioning myself as a psychologist: "I'll have to wear suits and nice dresses with blazers, so people won't mistake me for a secretary." She'd been offended by my statement; as secretary to a young, well-dressed female boss who belittled her and shook her confidence, she took it as a personal attack. But she'd let go of her resentment and accepted my remark as an expression of my own insecurity, not an indictment of her. That day was mine for shopping, and I loved it.

Choosing dresses and cutting my hair with Mom's preferences in mind are subtle gestures. I wonder if she sees them as the gifts I intend them to be.

I am not the only one bringing presents. The doorbell rings, and I find the hands of friends or health-care workers or delivery people outstretched with flowers and casseroles, a more comfortable bed, homemade soup. Long-distance friends send cards, photos, nutritional supplements, and call on the phone. I relay each gift to my mother, and her gratitude flows like water. But though she admires the food, joins the conversations, and tries to eat, her attention is shifting away from the material toward life's essence.

And she is worrying about what comes next.

Finally I am beginning to understand.

While I have been focusing on how to help my mother recover enough to do all her favorite things in life one last time, she has been focusing on just one thing—dying—and how to do it for the first and only time.

"This is Pastor Johnson, Mom. He is a Lutheran minister associated with the hospice and would like to talk with you. Would you like me to stay or leave to give you privacy?"

Mom shoots me a look of insistence, and says, "Stay," as the large chaplain in the black suit and clerical collar shakes her hand and holds it gently for a moment before sensing her discomfort and releasing it. He bends down slightly and keeps his elbows tight to his sides—habits designed, perhaps, to make him appear smaller than he is so as not to intimidate. He is kindly and not too pushy. But Mom is suspicious—she doesn't want someone asking if she's been born again or something. She keeps the conversation superficial, with one-word answers or humorous diversions. He doesn't strike me as being too pushy about religion, but he does respond to my mother's reticence by talking too much. By the time he leaves, I know Mom won't want to see him again.

"What did you think of him," I ask after he's gone.

"He's a nice enough person, but not someone I could really talk to."

I take from Mom's answer that she does want to talk to someone. "If you'd be interested in talking with someone else, there's a minister at my church who would come and see you. Her name is Margaret Anne Fohl. She's in her fifties and does a lot of pastoral counseling. I think you'd like her."

Mom agrees.

When Margaret Anne comes a few days later, she is dressed in a colorful floral skirt and a sweater—a nice contrast to her formal black church robes. Again I offer Mom privacy, but she urges me to stay. It takes Margaret Anne only a question or two—about Mom's thoughts about religion—to get Mom started. Though they've only met, Mom tells Margaret Anne her entire life story during the course of their conversation. And when she's said as much as she wants to about herself, they talk about feminism and the ordination of women. Mom is energized instead of tired at the end of their hour-long discussion.

The second meeting with Margaret Anne, a week later, is completely different from the first. This time Mom wants to talk about dying.

"What is the right way to die?" she asks.

"There are probably as many right ways to die as there are people," Margaret Anne replies. "What do you feel you should be doing?"

"Well, I feel like I'm supposed to be having deep, meaningful conversations with people, or feeling certain feelings. But I don't know if I'm doing that."

"You're doing just fine," Margaret Anne reassures after listening for a while.

Mom is open to conversations about dying with others as well. We are developing a sense of normalcy in talking about death—despite the societal taboos against open discussion of it. Death is a part of our daily lives now. And while it feels increasingly natural, it is never casual—each exchange is profound.

The next person Mom talks with about dying is Kenwyn. In the weeks since she arrived at our house, Kenwyn has taken an increasingly active role in caring for Mom. As soon as he comes home from work, he takes over transferring her in and out of the wheelchair to give my back a rest. He's worked out how to help Mom at night and with her personal care in a way that protects her privacy. She often asks for him to move her—trusting completely this son-in-law she once found so troubling. She tells him what a good father he is, and he shares with her his mother's experience of dying.

"I was with my mother for eight days just before she died," Kenwyn begins. "She was happy when I asked her how she felt about dying. Everyone else was tiptoeing around the subject."

Mom is caught up in the story, watching Kenwyn's face as he talks, her eyes transfixed with awe.

"I'll never forget what she said to me," Kenwyn continues. "She said, 'I feel like I'm about to begin the biggest adventure of my life!'"

"I wish I could believe something like that," Mom replied. "It must be so comforting."

Chapter 11

Sacred Water

As I help Mom prepare for bed, I can feel her anxiety snaking around my ankles. She slept on the couch in front of the TV for most of the afternoon, joined the family for dinner, and perked up for the prime-time shows. But as bedtime looms, she is less able to contain her pain and fear. Nighttime and my impending abandonment frighten her.

"I don't think I'll be able to fall asleep tonight, Sara. That aide doesn't know how to make me comfortable." It's been easier for me since we hired a night nursing aide, but Mom takes every opportunity to tell me she prefers my care to that of anyone else.

"I'll stay for a few minutes to make sure you're comfortable." I pull the rocking chair close to the bed. "You'll be all right."

Half-jokingly she whines, "I want my mother," and we both know that I'm the stand-in.

"When my children have trouble falling asleep, I tell them their birth stories. But I can't tell you the story of the day you were born, Mom. I wasn't there."

"No you weren't, but I was there the day you were born. I could tell you that."

"That would be great!" I'm surprised and delighted that in her childlike neediness, she can still offer to mother me. I don't mind that the story is more about her than me.

"I was so loony when I was pregnant with you," she begins.

I've heard the story many times and could tell the rest myself, but I just listen.

"I truly thought I was going insane. I couldn't stop crying and worrying. In those days, in rural Montana, doctors still made house calls. Dr. Bennett would sit beside me, pat my hand, and pass me tissues while I blubbered. He told me everything would be fine, that it was just hormones. And as soon as you were born, I was fine.

"The day I went into labor with you, my friend Barbara washed my hair for me."

My ears perk up. I haven't heard this detail before, and I realize that being washed figures in several stories my mother has told me recently. "The day Kevin was born, your father washed my feet for me," she'd said. "I'd been going around the apartment barefoot because my feet were swollen and my shoes didn't fit. I was so pregnant I hadn't been able to reach my feet for days. I couldn't show up at the hospital with dirty feet!" And a few nights ago, when we were talking about how she and my father met and about other boyfriends she'd had, she mentioned an engagement that evaporated, not long after it began, "to a man I met soon after getting out of the hospital. One night he asked me what I could and couldn't do since the polio, and when I mentioned needing help in the shower, the conversation petered out. After that he just stopped calling me. I never saw him again."

As I consider the shower not taken, the foot washing, the shampooing, and the wiping of tears alongside today's bed baths, wheelchair transfers, pillow plumping, and ointment rubbing, I am filled with admiration for my mother's graciousness in receiving. Could I endure dependency with such equanimity? I know how to give, but do I know how to rest in the care of another?

I notice that I'm no longer irritated when Mom's handling of her dependency isn't straightforward and clear. Only a few months ago, I cringed whenever her way of asking for help rubbed me the wrong way. I hated it when she said, "If you're going toward the kitchen, would you mind making a piece of toast for me?" as if I'd do it only if it were convenient.

I'm sure my father chose my mother not just because she was beautiful, witty, and intelligent, but because she needed him—he felt blessed by her abilities and her handicap. I know this because I feel it, too. Each time I lift or wash or feed or soothe, I experience the pleasure of helping. Each time the doorbell rings, I learn that I am not alone, that I am in the company of caring people. They climb my front porch steps to deliver food, flowers, mail, compassion, and companionship, because my mother is dying and I am grieving and they have something to offer.

Mom is calmer after our talk about birth. She thinks she may be able to sleep, but complains about the pain in her back. I offer to massage it before I say, "Good night, I love you," and head to bed.

My hands glisten with oil, and as I move them across my mother's back, they trail after-images, becoming many hands. They are my father's large hands tenderly washing his young wife's feet as she tenses with a contraction. They are Barbara's hands buried in a froth of shampoo as she lathers her friend's hair on the day I was born. They are the hands of a woman from church washing carrots for a pot of soup that she makes for us. Each hand is drenched in sacred water.

I am getting really good at taking care of Mom—perhaps too good. Two of her friends drive down from Rochester to spend time with Mom and give me a rest. Mary Lou and Fran are calm and confident as they offer to look after Mom while I go to church.

As soon as we get home from church, I wander around the yard and find myself attracted to a large, prickly bush. "I bet this bush hasn't been pruned in the ten years we've lived here!" I say to myself, cutting away at dead branches with unreasonable glee. "I can't believe what a mess it is!" It is a hot day, and I am enjoying the distraction of physical exertion and of the danger involved in moving further into the bush without the protection of long pants or gardening gloves. I look up with annoyance when Mary Lou calls from the front porch.

"Your mother is wondering when you are coming in," she says politely.

I am sweaty, scratched, and mud-stained, and far from finished with my impromptu project. "What does she need?" I ask, not so politely.

"She's just missing you, I think. We're doing what we can to respond to her needs, but she likes the way you take care of her best."

Toward the end of the month, the pace of life accelerates, despite our wish for time and peace to accommodate dying. Aunt Cis, Mom's only sibling, is flying in from Chicago to see her for the first time since the cancer was diagnosed. I worry that she doesn't realize how little time Mom has left; she keeps reminding me that this is her first trip to Philadelphia, as if we'll be touring the historic district in a horse-drawn carriage and snapping pictures of the Liberty Bell. I'm thankful Mom's pathologist friend, Dawn, is coming for the weekend; she makes it clear that she's coming to support me as much as to visit Mom. A group of staff members from the day-care center will stop by on Sunday, en route from a demonstration in Washington, D.C., for the needs and rights of children. They plan to present an award to Mom.

In addition to the visitors who come to see my mother, Kenwyn and I have more than the average number of weekend events involving the children—two baseball games, a violin concert, a birthday party, three ballet rehearsals, and a recital. There are beds to make, meals to prepare, conversations to have, uniforms to wash, trousers to iron, costumes to alter, hair to pin up, presents to wrap, schedules to coordinate, chauffeuring to do, pictures to take, and accomplishments to acknowledge.

Dawn arrives Saturday morning, and with a sweeping glance, takes in the scene and gets to work. Her instincts are similar to mine, from the extra ingredients she adds to the vegetarian chili to her insights about the relationship between Mom and Aunt Cis; I'm comforted to know that the person who has volunteered to help fill my shoes this weekend wears exactly my size.

I try to step back from Mom, creating space for her visitors to connect with her through caring and companionship. I remain alert to her energies and emotions, however, and facilitate interactions when they founder. She asks, in a tone of exasperation reserved for conversations about her chronologically older but, in her eyes, emotionally younger sister, "Does Cis have any clue about what's going on here?" I say: "Why don't you ask her? She's right here," knowing that Aunt Cis is keenly aware that her sister is dying but reluctant to initiate a conversation about it. For the first time since the surgery, Mom suggests that I leave the room, and she and Cis talk in private. After only a few minutes, Cis comes to find me to say that my mother needs me and that their short exchange was simple but deeply satisfying.

I am needed to grease the wheels of communication when the day-care staff arrive, bringing a plaque engraved with "The Jane K. Corse Award for Staff Excellence."

"We present this award to you, Jane, in honor of your profound contribution to Asbury Day Care Center over the last sixteen years," Karen, the director, begins. "You are the 1996 recipient. It will be given each year to a member of the staff or board who most exemplifies your dedication and compassion. It is one small way we can acknowledge how much you have given to us. We will miss you."

I am deeply moved to witness my mother honored in this way; I'm not the only person crying. But Mom's face is as still as a stone—she looks so alone on the couch. I move to sit next to her and put an arm around her shoulders; my action creates a release. "It's hard for me to express any emotion these days," she explains to us in a monotone. "But that doesn't mean I'm not very moved."

Mom seems exhausted. I invite everyone to the dining room for brunch, and she decides to rest on the couch. "Would you like to say good-bye to people now or when they're ready to leave?"

"Let me talk to Karen now." I guess she's ready to say some good-byes.

After the day-care crew leaves, Kenwyn and I take Aunt Cis to see Kalila's ballet performance. It is a drawn-out affair in a crowded and airless theater; we are stifling in the early June heat as we watch the dance programs, waiting for the three-minute segment featuring Kalila's class. Kenwyn volunteers to leave before Kalila appears, to enable the aide who is taking care of Mom to move on to her next commitment. When I get home, he tells me about their conversation.

"I asked your mother how she's doing. Actually, I used the word *dying*. I asked her how she's dying. She said, 'They'd better get here soon if they want to say good-bye to me.' When I asked her who she meant, she said Kevin, Jen, and Connie. When I said that they were all planning to come sometime next weekend, she said, 'Oh, that'll be too late.'"

I am frightened into action. One of the most nerve-wracking responsibilities as Mom's caregiver is advising her friends and family about her condition, making judgments about how much time she might have before she dies, and helping people decide when to visit. For the last couple of weeks, Jen has been asking me when she should come down, and I tell her that we're doing fine, that I'll let her know when I need the help or it's getting close. The last time we talked, Jen pushed me. "Why do you keep telling me not to come down?" And though I told her I wasn't trying to keep her away, I admitted that I liked being the one in charge.

Now I wonder if I've waited too long . . . out of what? A stubborn desire to prove that I can handle this alone? An unwillingness to admit that Mom may never have the "good weeks" I thought she'd enjoy once she stopped worrying about who would care for her? An inability to accept that she is closer to death than I thought?

I call my siblings and Connie, and encourage them to come earlier than planned. My conversation with Kevin and Tina is the most difficult. I discover that they've postponed their trip by another week, that Tina has been advised not to come because of her late stage of pregnancy, and that four-year-old Teija will come instead. I can sense their struggle to track what's happening from three thousand miles away. Tina recently asked me where I thought Mom would spend Thanksgiving, more than six months from now, and I'm calling to suggest that she may not make it to next week, much less to early July, when their second child will be born. "Two weeks from now might be too late," I caution, "and seeing Mom might be too much of a shock for Teija. It's hard on my kids, who are older and have watched her gradually get worse over the last couple of months." Later Kevin calls with a new arrival time and the decision to come alone.

Mom is relieved to know that people are on their way.

The next day I help Mom with her morning routine—exercises, sips of ginger ale, choosing clothes for the day—and Cis keeps us company. Valerie, Mom's morning aide, will arrive soon. Mom looks forward to seeing Valerie each day. She got over her first reaction of, "Gee, you're pretty small; you won't be able to lift me," as soon as Valerie said, "It just takes a good, solid hug," and putting her arms around Mom's waist, swung her easily into the wheelchair. Now Mom calls Valerie her hugging lady, and Valerie always comments on Mom's dignity and courage.

"I'm going out to do some shopping," I tell Mom when Valerie arrives. "I'll see if I can find a bedpan for you." She's been asking for one; the commode is getting harder to use.

"Oh, let me come with you," Cis says, grabbing her purse. "I'd like to buy the bedpan for your mother."

I am touched profoundly by a sister's last gift—a mustard-yellow molded plastic bedpan, retailing for $3.99 plus tax.

In the evening I help the new night aide, Winette, settle Mom into bed. Winette has been coming since Thursday, and

Mom seems to like her much better than the previous aide. "I didn't want to trouble you with the burden of finding someone new, so I didn't say anything for a long time. But it's nice to have someone who doesn't make me wait when I need something and isn't gruff with me." The other aide had been polite around me; I hadn't wanted to hear that she wasn't nice to Mom. I'm glad I finally asked for a different aide.

While I'm in the bathroom rinsing a washcloth, Mom calls: "Sara, come here. I want to talk to you."

"Oh, dear. What have I done?" is my immediate reaction. I don't want to find out, but I go anyway.

"I feel good about the things we worked out today," she begins. "I like Winette, and I'm glad you got the bedpan. Bringing me ice chips to suck really helps my dry mouth and sore throat. I just wanted to tell you how grateful I am for everything."

I squeeze Mom's hand. How ridiculous I am to assume that she's mad at me!

Mom is sitting up in bed, washed, dressed, and bristling with energy. Winette greets me on her way to empty the bedpan, and Aunt Cis rocks in the chair by the bed, bleary-eyed in her nightgown. This much activity so early in the morning runs counter to all the rhythms we've established in the last month.

"My, you're up early!" I remark.

"I asked to get washed and dressed a couple of hours ago." My mother, the night owl, awake at five o'clock in the morning?

"Don't you want to sleep a little longer?"

"Oh, I didn't sleep at all last night." She is unperturbed.

I glance at Winette.

"That's right. Your mother was awake all night, talking."

"Talking?"

Winette shrugs and shakes her head to halt my probing.

The energy in the room feels electrically charged; it makes me edgy.

The dog notices, too. Instead of sniffing around the room in a cursory way and curling up for a nap, he's sitting at attention at the end of the bed, ears alert, eyes steady on Mom. He doesn't seem disturbed, though, by whatever he's noticing.

"Sara, I think I lost the schedule."

"What schedule, Mom?" Does she mean her daily routine? She has lost that, it seems.

"Well, what time does Kevin's plane arrive?"

"Oh, Kevin isn't coming until Thursday morning. It's Cis who's flying today. Her plane leaves at two o'clock. And Jen's coming tonight, and Connie tomorrow."

Valerie, the hugging lady, arrives, and laughs warmly when she sees Mom. "Aren't you the early bird, washed and dressed already!" she says, giving Mom a squeeze. "Have you done your exercises?"

"No, I decided to skip them today."

Valerie nods knowingly. "I'll just change your bed then, after we get you settled in the wheelchair to go into the living room."

Before she leaves, Tracy, the hospice nurse, comes to check Mom's vital signs and a skin irritation that Valerie points out. Mom has fewer physical complaints than usual.

"How was your weekend?" Tracy asks.

"Busy," Mom says. "Too busy."

"It was a big weekend," I add. "Nonstop activity and lots of visitors. Why don't you tell Valerie and Tracy about the Jane Corse Award."

"What?"

"Don't you remember? Karen presented you with the Jane Corse Award for Staff Excellence."

"Karen?"

"You know Karen. She's been your boss at the day-care center for the last few years."

"Oh, yes, Karen. Actually, she's been my boss the whole time I've been at the center."

"I don't think so, Mom. Karen's only had that position for the last five years or so."

"No, Karen has always been my boss."

"What about Jean? Wasn't she your first boss? And then there was Patricia."

"I don't know about that. It's always been Karen."

I shouldn't persist, but this bothers me more than anything else I've seen or heard this morning. It's not like her to forget things like that. I tell Valerie and Tracy about Mom's role at the day-care center, how she was the glue that held the center together.

"That's great, Jane," says Valerie. "Are you ready to go?"

I pull Tracy aside as Valerie wheels Mom out of the room. "How will I know if she's about to die? Do I call you or the doctor?"

"You can call me if you want help or support. The doctor knows your mother's status. He just needs to be informed when she dies. Have you chosen a funeral home?"

"No, I haven't even thought about it. Mom wants her body cremated. Do I look in the yellow pages? That seems so cold."

Aunt Cis is nervous about making it to the airport, so I call a cab and set her bags by the door. "I'm glad you came this weekend. Sorry you didn't get to see much of Philadelphia."

"Not even the Liberty Bell. But it doesn't matter."

"Hold on," I say, and race off to find the little bell I'd set on Mom's night table. "This may be the closest you ever get to it."

Aunt Cis giggles, examines the little bronze replica, jingles it, slips it in her purse, and says, "Thanks!" My eyes widen. I brought it to show her, not intending to give Phillip's souvenir away. He'd been so eager to go to Independence Mall when his first-grade class was studying Philadelphia history; to buy the bell, a quill pen, and parchment paper; and to cast us as the founding fathers in his reenactment of the signing of the Declaration of Independence. But I can't ask her to give it back.

Cis's cab arrives, and I am alone with Mom for the first time in four days.

Chapter 12

Angels and Spirits

Mom lies on the couch, her eyes half-closed to white slits, her mouth moving in a soft mumble. I strain to hear, but the words are a jumble, with only an occasional recognizable phrase.

"Are you okay, Mom?" I ask when she moans.

She doesn't answer.

"Mom, are you okay? Can I get you something?"

"What?"

"Do you need anything? What were you saying?"

"Oh, I wasn't talking to you."

"Who were you talking to, Mom?"

"There are angels and spirits that you cannot see." She gestures loosely toward the center of the room.

I feel alone and frightened. It is hours until the hospice volunteer will come. I sit beside Mom, watching her mouth move, her chest rise with each breath, and her hands pluck at the quilt as if she is picking blueberries. I should . . . I should keep vigil. Should I keep vigil? I can't stand doing nothing. I pick up a book, but stop when I realize that I've read the same sentence twelve times. I go to the kitchen, load a few dishes in the dishwasher, hurry back to peek at Mom, swipe dust off the windowsill, look out the window at the potato chip bags, candy wrappers, and dead leaves blown against the side fence, and wonder who will clear them away. I again read the handout Mary Lou brought us from the hospice where she works. It describes what to expect as someone nears death, from signs that are apparent a month or two before, such as changes in appetite and energy, to those that appear in the last days, hours, and minutes, such as the plucking Mom is doing, changes in breathing, sometimes coma.

I check on Mom again.

What if Mom dies in the next few hours, when I'm alone with her and don't know what to do? What if Kevin and Jen don't make it here before she dies?

I try sitting with her again, thumbing through a catalogue. Somehow I tolerate the tension, and at three o'clock the doorbell rings. It is Sister Andrea, the coordinator of hospice volunteers.

"Your regular volunteer couldn't come today, so I came myself."

"Thank you! I'm having a horrible day. I don't know what is happening with Mom, but I'm so afraid she's going to die. She's acting so differently today. And I need to get the kids from school. Will you be okay with Mom? Can you lift her? She used the commode recently. I don't think she'll need to be moved, but she might."

"Your mother and I will be fine while you're gone. We'll be just fine."

"It's not that I can't deal with Mom's dying," I blurt out. "I know she's dying. But what if my brother and sister don't make it here to see her before she goes? Jen should be here by now; I don't know what's taking her so long. But Kevin isn't coming until Thursday. It might be too late! What if I've waited too long?"

"It's okay, Sara, it's all going to be okay. It's not within your power to make it be a certain way for everyone, but it's going to be okay."

"Okay. It'll be okay," I leave the house repeating this new mantra. "Whatever happens, it'll be okay."

It's been three days since Mom slept. She rarely seems fully awake, but she talks continually. I strain to pay attention to her endless string of speech, convinced that she will let loose with some profound truth about the universe or God or the meaning of life. But her voice is soft, and though I can understand some words and phrases, I forget them in the effort to hear what's coming next.

When Jen arrives on Tuesday night, I heave a sigh of relief. After many hours of worrying that she will die before the rest of the family gathers, I begin to relax and prepare to share the burden. I slip upstairs to read a bedtime story to the children, leaving Mom and Jen in front of the television, but I soon hear Mom bristling about the change in caregivers. "I need a bowl; I feel queasy," she calls, and when Jen rushes from the kitchen with a bowl, her tone grows harsh. "That's not the one I use; that's too small. Where's the plastic one? Where's Sara?"

Jen is hurt by Mom's reaction, but she eases into a caring role and discovers her special gifts. While I find it increasingly difficult to follow what Mom is saying, Jen has an uncanny ability to understand her rambling speech and becomes the translator. After I go to bed, she sits in the rocking chair, holds Mom's hand, and hopes for the kind of healing conversations Mom and I were able to have only last week. "She speaks more clearly at night," Jen observes. But the articulate has been crowded out by the cryptic, and so she decodes. "Mom's angels and spirits seem to be moving close enough for her to recognize. I heard her say 'Delores.' Maybe she sees her friend who committed suicide. I think she sees Dad, too. Last night she suddenly said, quite clearly: 'Why did you leave me? I've been so lonely!'"

On Wednesday afternoon Connie arrives and slips smoothly into the role of family supporter, and on Thursday morning, I check in on Mom and Jen and Connie before leaving for the airport to meet Kevin's plane.

Mom's speech is rolling, repetitious, and agitated; she repeats first a pair of words, and then just one, over and over. "I asked Mom how she's doing, and she said, 'I'm chanting,'" Jen explains.

"I think she's struggling to hang on until Kevin gets here," Connie says gently.

When Kevin arrives Mom interrupts her chanting. Her demeanor changes as she holds his hand, receives his hug, and speaks to him. "I heard her say, 'I love you' and 'I'm sorry,'" Jen asserts, but to Kevin's ears, it is only a mumble. Mom doesn't seem to focus her eyes on anything, and he's not sure he's been recognized. "She knows it's you," Connie affirms. "You made it in time. You've given her a wonderful gift."

Mom's voice is hoarse, and her breath rattles through her chest. She isn't in pain or emotional distress, and her body is fairly quiet, but she appears to be working very hard; just listening to her makes me feel exhausted. From all my reading and talking with hospice workers and nurses, I have been expecting Mom to become silent, to slip into a coma. Instead she is talking. It is as if she is narrating her dying, bringing us with her as far as she can take us.

The curtain between life and death is a gossamer veil. I cannot see through it, but Mom offers a glimpse with her talk of light and lightness, angels and spirits, gratitude and love. Although I have been thinking of myself as a midwife to my mother's next birthing, a comforter during her transition from matter to spirit, I, too, am comforted. I have the sense that there are midwives on the other side, that we do not make the journey alone.

At about one o'clock, Kevin, Jen, and I drift from Mom's bedside for a short break, leaving Connie to keep watch. Jen lies down for a nap; she slept little last night, and feels a migraine coming on. Kevin dozes on the couch next to Mom, groggy from his red-eye flight. I make myself some lunch, page through a picture book about the death of a grandparent, and read passages over the phone to my friend Pat.

"Sara, come quickly! I think she's going!" Connie rushes through the kitchen, calling out to me.

"I've got to go, Pat." I drop the cordless phone and race after Connie.

The midday sun streams through Mom's window, glinting off the steel rails of the hospital bed and lighting up Kalila's collage of pink, purple, green, and yellow tissue-paper flowers like a stained-glass window. Jen leans over the bed. Kevin perches on the edge of the couch, his hand resting on the bedclothes. Connie moves around the rocking chair to the head of the bed; I stand at its foot. Mom lies so still on the bed.

I watch to see if she is breathing, holding my own breath. For the first time in more than forty-eight hours, the room is silent, devoid of Mom's raspy mumbling, her chanting, and the deep rattling of her breathing. We startle when she suddenly exhales—exhalation without inhalation.

She exhales two more times.

The skin on her hand flattens, coming to rest on bone.

"Three parting breaths," Connie says softly. "One for each of you."

A moment passes before I risk an exhale.

When I finally take a deep breath, it is to move into action again, unable after all those weeks to sit still, even long enough for the reality of my mother's death to sink in. "I guess I should call the hospice," I say. "Tracy's instructions were to let her know when Mom died. She said she has to ask me some questions."

When Tracy answers the phone, I tell her the news in a matter-of-fact way.

"Oh, I'm so sorry," she says gently. "When did it happen?"

I answer this simple question and wait for the next, but she is silent.

"Didn't you say you had some questions you needed to ask me?" I prompt. I've been curious about those for several days.

"Well, usually when I get this kind of call, the family member is upset and uncertain about whether or not the person is dead. I ask them questions to help them identify that," Tracy explains.

"Well, she's just laying there looking pretty dead," I say without thinking, and Kevin, Jen, and Connie, lined up on the couch listening to my side of the conversation, burst out laughing.

"I'm sorry," I apologize, as Tracy joins the laughter.

"It's perfectly fine," Tracy reassures me. I can hear another voice in the background, and realize that she isn't talking to me alone. "I'm at home right now, and my husband is looking at me as if I am crazy for laughing at a time like this. But humor is often a part of the mix."

Although there is a sense of calm in the room, the shocking energy of loss swirls around us all, looking for an outlet, as willing to escape in laughter as in wailing or tears. It's as if we are blanketed by an emotional crazy quilt.

Once we recover Tracy asks if we've chosen a funeral home yet.

"No, do we have to call right away?" I look at my watch. "I don't want her whisked away before Kenwyn and the children come home.

"It's best to place the call now," Tracy advises. "You can tell them how much time you need."

I call Kenwyn and then a funeral home. "We'll be there in fifteen minutes," the man in the office announces.

"No, that's too soon," I panic. "Can you come a little later? I'll call you."

Having embraced my mother's dying at home, I am loath to release her body to the undertaker.

"We should prepare Mom's body," I suggest. But after dabbing a warm washcloth at the corner of her mouth and combing her hair, there seems to be nothing else to do. I call the funeral home again, and ask them to come in an hour.

Kenwyn rides his bicycle home from his office in less than ten minutes, and we jump in the car to collect the children from school. It is a few minutes before dismissal on the second to last day of the school year, and teachers are distributing the fruits of the year's labors. Kalila balances a clay pot on a pile of self-published books. I spot the bright pink cover of a counting book that she shared with me at last month's "Meet the Author Day"—I remember my favorite page was "nine girls trampolining." Kalila doesn't question my early arrival, but shoots me an occasional sidelong glance as I hustle her out to the car. Kenwyn and the boys are already climbing in the car.

"Grandma died a little while ago, very peacefully," I explain as we pause in the parking lot. "Her body is lying on her bed at home."

The children are silent. No one asks a question or cries.

"Some people find it helpful to look at the body of the person who has died, because it helps them to understand and accept the death. Other people would rather remember the person as they were when they were alive. You can choose what you want to do," I explain.

"I guess I'll look at Grandma's body," Justin announces.

"Me, too," says Phillip.

Kalila pages through a book that she has pulled out of her backpack.

"What about you, sweetie," I prompt. "Would you rather look at Grandma's body or remember her as she was when she was alive."

"To remember her alive," she mumbles.

When we arrive at our street corner and prepare to back into the driveway, I spot three young men standing near the front porch, looking hot and uncomfortable in their uniform of black pants and white shirts.

"Oh, no. They're here already," I say. The sight of them cracks my emotional armor.

"They've been here since a few minutes after you left," Kevin explains as we tumble out of the car. "We made them wait outside."

"Good," I snarl. I feel an unreasonable burst of hostility toward these men who want to rush my mother out of my home.

Kalila runs to the swing set in the backyard while Phillip, Justin, Kenwyn, and I circle Mom's bed. Connie, Jen, and Kevin step out to give us privacy.

"Let's say a prayer for Grandma," I suggest. "I'll start, and you can each join in." We end the prayer by holding hands and squeezing, a ritual the children learned at their Quaker school, to symbolize God's love moving through us and encircling us, and we release her. The boys join Kalila on the swing set, and someone nods to the men in the white shirts and black pants.

I make myself watch as the men walk in with a large, black bag—a body bag. Can't they fold a soft, white shroud around her? Does it have to be like this? Only a few days ago, I read that more than eighty percent of deaths take place in a hospital; fewer than twenty percent happen at home. We have been saved from a certain kind of trauma—the clattering wheels of hospital gurneys, the paged announcements summoning staff to the room, the caring arm around the shoulder leading us away. What we have been able to give Mom has felt so natural and right. It is only this carrying out of her body, past the curious eyes of neighbors, that feels brutal.

But at the same time, that body is not my mother anymore. Her spirit has flown.

Suddenly it feels as if I have nothing to do. I have been working so hard for the last several weeks to hold everything together; now I am like a cartoon character running full speed off the edge of a cliff: my legs are churning still, and I brace for the sudden plunge to the bottom of the cavern. But instead of crashing, I am buoyed by the angels, the midwives, the friends, the spirits—earthly and holy—that have gathered to help Mom's passing. A pan of lasagna arrives, then a cake, and more flowers. Kevin, Jen, and Connie call Mom's friends, write an obituary, and organize a funeral. The day-care center plans a reception. Kevin dons the mantle of executor of the will. He gives me a book titled *Motherless Daughters,* by Hope Edelman. "Dear Sara," it says on the flyleaf, "Thank you for taking care of our mother." Each time the doorbell rings or the phone jangles or I pick up that book and read the inscription or someone hugs me, I loosen the grip of self-reliance, and I experience God's healing grace embodied in each act of love, nestling me in a cushion of care.

If I expected my mother's death to bring the sudden aching wrench of grief that grabbed me when my father died, I was wrong. This time my grieving has been prolonged and gradual and gentle. The sadness of loss is tempered by the celebration of a transformation in our relationship and a healing within me. Together Mom and I have counteracted two lifetimes' worth—hers and mine—of asking, needing, and wanting. In surrendering to her lifelong wish to be taken care of, I am fulfilled.

I am filled full.

Epilogue

August 1996

In the weeks after my mother died, Kalila became a "Velcro" girl, three feet tall and clinging to my side, terrified to let me out of her sight.

"Mom!" she'd yell, voice edgy with panic, whenever she noticed that I wasn't right beside her. Even while engrossed in watching a favorite video or playing with a friend, she called out for me at five-minute intervals. Every day. Day after day.

"I'm right here, Kalila. What do you want?" I'd answer from the kitchen or the bathroom or even from the same room as she, responding calmly to her unceasing requests for reassurance of my existence. Each call pulled me into the present, dragged me from the edge of sorrow, and reminded me that my daughter needed me here and now—much as her grandmother had needed me.

Kalila was easily comforted. As soon as she heard my voice and knew where I was, she said, "Nothing" or "Never mind" or "Just to be sure," and turned back to playing for another few minutes.

After a while we dropped the variations—it was always "I'm right here" and "Just to be sure." A rhythmic call and response. A prayer.

I was grateful for an Adirondack summer and a leave of absence from work for the opportunity to give over to Kalila's needs. When I focused on her fears, I didn't notice how my own senses were dulled by exhaustion and grief to the beauty of the sunlight sparkling on Long Lake and the mountains rising behind.

Then one day Kalila put her terror into words. "I don't want you to disappear."

How can you tell your child that you won't disappear? I offered her what consolation I could, but tapping into her primal fear reminded me of my own fear of dying, of being called on to support and soothe someone else as they died, of experiencing another loss. How would I ever have the strength to deal with another death?

That night I lay awake long after Kenwyn fell asleep beside me. I knew Kalila was going to be okay—already she was stretching to ten minutes the time between calls to check on me. But what of me? Would I be okay? And if not, who would comfort me?

Moonlight streamed across my pillow, and with it came a deep sense of peace. I felt God's answer to my version of Kalila's prayer—the divine "I am here."

I pulled myself up on one elbow and placed my hand lightly on Kenwyn's forehead. "I'll take care of you," I promised him as he slept. "If anything should happen to you, I'll take care of you."

Perhaps it seems like a strange way to express God's loving presence in my life—to assure my sleeping husband that I would hold him if he needed me. But I sensed God's hand brushing back my fears, giving me courage, holding me. I felt safe, not because I thought that nothing bad would ever happen again, but because I realized that love had been there all along, carrying us through troubled times, sending people to help, healing us.

In that moment of restful peace, I again searched my heart for the hole that first appeared when my father died. For so many years, that wound throbbed with a persistent ache, despite all my tears and talk, my efforts to grieve and let go and move on. I'd long since resigned myself to the idea that this dull pain, waxing and waning, was an expected and irreparable consequence of losing a beloved parent, and would be with me for life. The day I learned that my mother had incurable cancer, I predicted the effect her death would have on me by using a simple mathematical formula: the hole in my heart would double in size. It would ache twice as much. I was certain.

Yet in the weeks following Mom's death, after the hugs and flowers and songs and poems were offered in celebration of her life, and the intense energy of caring and dying dissipated, I kept an eye out for the hole in my heart that I expected to grow bigger and throb more acutely. But I found no bigger hole; there was no heightened pain. Although her death brought sadness and loss, we had taken the time to do the work of good-bye, and I didn't feel the same wrenching pain, the disbelief, and the lack of resolution that I felt with my father's sudden death. In embracing my mother's dying, I opened myself to the love and healing that accompanied us.

My mathematical formula had been wrong.

I had been wrong about something else as well. What I had learned in the past about recovering from grief—from walking through it myself, from studying it, and from helping others—was limited to the psychological and the physical. I had no idea that something greater was in store. But with all the poking around in my heart to find new wounds, I was surprised to realize that I couldn't find the old familiar hole either. Instead of aching with greater loss, my long-wounded heart was healed. Spiritually, by grace.

October 2003

"This time, as you set up for your spin, reach out with your arms and find the energy generated by your windup," my coach instructs. "Imagine that you're trying to get your arms around a big teddy bear. Grab on to that energy, and hug it firmly to generate speed."

As I step into the spin, I search for the big bear. Finding the tension, I haul it toward my chest and accelerate. I stand firm, controlling the speed.

"Step out of it, *now!*" my coach calls as I'm still spinning. He is no longer happy for me to wind down to a gentle sigh, but asks me to stretch out into the landing position and stroke forward despite my dizziness. "Practice going straight into the next moves in your program."

Centering a spin is not the elusive mystery it once was, nor is claiming space on the ice or taking a leap of faith. I center my spins more often than not, and now what absorbs me is the interplay of strength, speed, and control. There is still calm at the center of a spin, but it is not a place of rest or retreat. It is filled with dynamic vitality, forces to liberate and to use.

My mother and I found the calm at the center as we became fully present to caring and to dying. And we were not alone. Daughter mothering mother mothering daughter—we were cradled all the while in the strong arms of God, the Great Mother.

I am nestled in those arms still. Centered in that peace, I notice what vibrant energy is created there, and the path is clear. We all are called to enact the transforming power of love, to release the divine in our midst.

Other Resources from Augsburg

Grieving the Death of a Mother by Harold Ivan Smith
144 pages, 0-8066-4347-1

Drawing on his own experience of loss, as well as those of others, Harold Ivan Smith guides readers through their grief, from the process of dying through the acts of remembering and honoring a mother after her death.

On Grieving the Death of a Father by Harold Ivan Smith
144 pages, 0-8066-2714-X

Smith has combined personal stories from Frederick Buechner, Norman Vincent Peale, Corrie ten Boom, James Dobson, and many other well-known people to help others through their grieving process.

When a Loved One Dies by Philip W. Williams
96 pages, 0-8066-4269-6

Philip W. Williams walks with you on the journey, helping you understand the confusing emotions and offering wisdom and insight from others who have lost a loved one. More important, he reminds you that God is always by your side, providing guidance, comfort, and strength.

When Your Parent Dies by Ron Klug
48 pages, 0-8066-4263-7

Even when the death is expected, the loss of a parent presents both unique challenges and opportunities for personal spiritual growth. This is a brief, focused book that guides adults through this difficult time. The author shows how the resources of faith can help a grieving person move forward in life to find hope and healing.

Available wherever books are sold.